Foreign Agents

Foreign Agents:

The American Israel Public Affairs
Committee from the 1963 Fulbright
Hearings to the 2005 Espionage
Scandal

by Grant F. Smith

Published by the Institute for Research: Middle Eastern Policy, Inc.
Calvert Station
PO Box 32041
Washington, DC 20007

First published in 2007 by the Institute for Research: Middle Eastern Policy

7 9 10 8 6
Copyright Institute for Research: Middle Eastern Policy, Inc.
All Rights Reserved

Hardcover ISBN-13: 978-0-9764437-8-0
Hardcover ISBN-10: 0-9764437-8-3

Library of Congress Cataloging-in-Publication Data

Smith, Grant F.
Foreign agents : the American Israel Public Affairs Committee from the 1963
Fulbright hearings to the 2005 espionage scandal / by Grant F. Smith.
    p. cm.
Includes index.
Paperback ISBN-13: 978-0-9764437-7-3 (alk. paper)
Paperback ISBN-10: 0-9764437-7-5
1. American Israel Public Affairs Committee. 2. Zionists--United States--
Political activity. 3. United States--Foreign relations--Israel. 4. Israel--Foreign
relations--United States. 5. United States--Foreign relations--1945-1989. 6.
United States--Foreign relations--1989- I. Title.
E184.36.P64S64 2007
327.7305694--dc22
                    2007027586

"A lobby is like a night flower: It thrives in the dark and dies in the sun."

Steve J. Rosen, AIPAC Director of Policy [1]

"Law is the essential foundation of stability and order both within societies and in international relations. As a conservative power, the United States has a vital interest in upholding and expanding the reign of law in international relations. Insofar as international law is observed, it provides us with stability and order and with a means of predicting the behavior of those with whom we have reciprocal legal obligations. When we violate the law ourselves, whatever short-term advantage may be gained, we are obviously encouraging others to violate the law; we thus encourage disorder and instability and thereby do incalculable damage to our own long-term interests."

Senator James William Fulbright [2]

Table of Contents

Table of Exhibits

About the Author

Grant F. Smith is director of research at the Washington, DC-based Institute for Research: Middle Eastern Policy (IRmep). Smith's research and analysis about US policy formulation, trade, opportunity costs, and international business strategy have appeared in the *Financial Times of London, Reuters, Inc. Magazine, Arab News, Kiplinger, Gannet, The Wall Street Journal, Al-Eqtisadiah, Khaleej Times,* the *New York Times,* the *Daily Star,* the Associated Press, and specialty publications such as the US State Department's *Washington File.* Smith has appeared on Voice of America (VOA) television, the BBC, Radio France Internationale, C-SPAN, Al Jazeera, and CNN, as well as numerous public radio programs. He is the author of the books *Deadly Dogma* (2006) and *Visa Denied* (2007) dealing with US Middle East policies and how they affect conflict, bilateral trade, investment, and job creation. He is the editor of the book *Neocon Middle East Policy,* derived from a 2003 IRmep policy symposium held in the Rayburn House Office building on Capitol Hill about a 1996 neoconservative plan for involving the US military more deeply across the Middle East.

Smith's research has taken him to more than 40 countries on assignments ranging from as little as a few days in length to a half-decade. Before joining IRmep, he was a senior analyst and later a program manager and consultant at the Boston-based Yankee Group Research, Inc. At Yankee Group, he worked on foreign direct investments of over $3 billion in development projects in 30 countries in conjunction with NGOs, investment banks, and both state-owned and private corporations.

Before that, Smith was marketing manager at the Minneapolis-based Investors Diversified Services (IDS), now Ameriprise Financial Advisors. Smith's formal education includes a BA in International Relations from the University of Minnesota and a master's degree in International Management from the University of St. Thomas in St. Paul, Minnesota. Smith's career in research includes the authorship of over 170 research papers, articles, surveys, and editorials on international issues.

Preface

The American Israel Public Affairs Committee (AIPAC) operates within a murky nexus regulated by four important but seldom enforced US laws. The Logan Act was written to prohibit unauthorized diplomacy on the part of Americans with no official mandate to negotiate on behalf of the United States. Federal election laws prohibit individuals from making excessive contributions and prohibit nonprofit corporations from coordinating Political Action Committee funds nationally to support or defeat candidates for office. The Foreign Agents Registration Act, or FARA, requires disclosure of the activities of agents lobbying for a foreign principal in the US. Finally, the 1917 Espionage Act prohibits trafficking US national intelligence information in ways that can be used to "the injury of the United States or to the advantage of a foreign country."[3]

Lax US law enforcement has led to the horrifying realization of many outcomes these important laws sought to forestall. Illegally coordinated AstroTurf[4] Israel lobby PACs exercise undue influence over Congress; AIPAC officials alternately conduct unauthorized diplomacy and secretly thwart debate, diplomacy, and sensible United States policies; a vast informal intelligence network in the service of a foreign government, some of it visible, most not, siphons commercial and US government intelligence off to Israel; and unregistered foreign agents conduct ongoing Israeli government propaganda campaigns without proper legal disclosures. Lack of law enforcement has put the US Congress and the American people under the *de facto* influence of a powerful foreign interest.

AIPAC has serially violated these four laws. Pursuing its goals of influencing American policy through illegal means has required a level of operational secrecy and commitment to obfuscation and misdirection worthy of a large national intelligence agency. Indeed, many AIPAC activities have all the trappings of intelligence agency collection and covert operations. However, instances of AIPAC planting foreign national propaganda in the US news media, systematically scouring the US government for classified national intelligence and forwarding it to Israel, and swinging elections through smear, innuendo, and coordinated delivery of critical campaign donations have periodically come to light. AIPAC's leadership transformed from an openly registered foreign agent into the operative of a secretive political intelligence-gathering and covert operations powerhouse between the 1940s and the 1960s. Israeli government and proxy seed money flowed to AIPAC's parent, the American Zionist Committee, and financed the creation of AIPAC. This critical foreign support helped AIPAC grow into a self-sustaining but essentially Israeli-controlled entity.

Few mainstream corporate media journalists or researchers now dare to write exposés or delve too deeply into AIPAC's history and secret initiatives. Fortunately, this has not always been the case. In the past, even the

Washington Post and *New York Times* bravely took on aspects of AIPAC secret operations, publishing embarrassing internal memos that exposed AIPAC's lawbreaking and contempt for limits placed on both foreign lobbying and US campaign laws. A careful review of a half-century of news reporting, legal proceedings, testimony, and internal AIPAC documents reveals both the criminality of the organization and the radical lengths to which staffers, former associates, directors, and operatives have been willing to go to achieve their objectives. It also reveals the extent to which news organizations have stopped investigating AIPAC. It is now far more common for reporters and editors to protect their working relationships with AIPAC in order to preserve access to news tidbits and purloined intelligence delivered on "deep background".

AIPAC exists at the core of a constellation of organizations that make up the "Israel lobby" in the United States. The Israel lobby was recently defined by two eminent academics as a "loose coalition of individuals and organizations who actively work to steer US foreign policy in a pro-Israel direction."[5]

Because no comprehensive research focused on AIPAC's history of lawbreaking has recently been published, egregious violations of US laws have successfully been framed by AIPAC and its supporters as "the work of junior officers," "uncharacteristic of the organization," and "isolated events." The absence of critical outside research has served AIPAC well. In considering whether to charge AIPAC as a criminal conspirator in a recent high-profile case involving purloined US national defense information allegedly trafficked to Israel, former US Attorney Paul McNulty utilized the Department of Justice "Thompson Memorandum" guidelines for prosecuting corporate crime.[i] These guidelines established criteria for evaluating whether an organization should be charged with criminal wrongdoing. Among the key guidelines are:

1. *The nature and seriousness of the offense;*
2. *The pervasiveness of wrongdoing within the corporation, including any management culpability;*
3. *Any history of similar conduct by the corporation;*
4. *The corporation's timely, voluntary disclosure of wrongdoing and willingness to cooperate in the investigation of its agents, including waiver of corporate attorney-client privilege and work product protection;*
5. *The existence and adequacy of the corporations compliance program,*
6. *The corporations remedial actions (including, inter alia, discipline or termination of the wrongdoers),*
7. *Collateral consequences, such as harm to non-culpable shareholders, pensioners, and employees,*

---

[i] The "Thompson Memorandum" guidelines have since been superseded, as explored in Chapter 5.

8. *The adequacy of prosecution of the responsible individuals and*
9. *The adequacy of civil remediation.*[6]

Documented AIPAC crimes up to the present day reveal that the organization has repeatedly failed most Thompson Memorandum guidelines. Nevertheless, the corporation itself has never been indicted for wrongdoing. Lack of information may be one reason. If a precise, detailed history of AIPAC crime had been readily available to McNulty when he was a US attorney, there is a possibility that the organization itself would have been indicted and faced a quick demise, à la Arthur Anderson or Enron, in the year 2005 if not earlier. However, no recent contextual history of AIPAC's origin and its criminal activity up to the 2005 espionage scandal has been published—until now.

One: US Lobby Startup Funding from Israel

AIPAC was founded by Isaiah L. "Si" Kenen, springing from the American Zionist Committee for Public Affairs. Kenen registered twice with the US Department of Justice under the Foreign Agent Registration Act (FARA) as a foreign agent for Israel.[7] On April 21, 1947 he registered as an agent of the American Section of the Jewish Agency for Israel.[8] Si Kenen also registered at FARA as an agent for the "Israel Information Services" on October 12, 1948 through May 13, 1951.[9] Kenen changed the committee's name from the American Zionist Committee for Public Affairs to the American Israel Public Affairs Committee in 1959, to better reflect that it, according to him, "raised its funds from both Zionists and non-Zionists."[10] Kenen's emphasis on a low-key, uncontroversial, and even non-descriptive organization name continued after his departure when AIPAC spawned a network of obliquely named political action committees (PACs) across the United States designed to sway the results of key elections. From a historical perspective, all of the lessons Kenen learned running the American Zionist Council with funds and guidance from the Israeli government are part of AIPAC's "institutional DNA." **It is impossible to understand AIPAC without understanding its precursor, the American Zionist Council.**

Kenen served as AIPAC's executive director and also owned and edited the influential newsletter, the *Near East Report*.[11] The *Near East Report* is now housed under a separate nonprofit corporate affiliate structure, for reasons explored later. Kenen was an Ohio newspaperman until 1943, when he left to become the secretary of the American Jewish Conference; he remained there until 1948.[12] He was also the Jewish Agency's information director between 1947 and 1948 at the United Nations. This was Israel's first UN delegation after its formation as a state in 1948. In 1951, Kenen went to Washington to lobby Congress for aid to Israel, founding the American Zionist Committee, which later spun off AIPAC. Between 1951 and March 15, 1954, Kenen directed legislative activity in Washington on behalf of the American Zionist Council. The American Zionist Council restructured its lobbying activities beginning in early 1954, when the organization's leaders became uncomfortable using internationally sourced tax-exempt donations for lobbying on Capitol Hill. Fred Scribner, a friendly US Undersecretary of Treasury, confidentially recommended during a 1959 meeting with key Zionist organizations operating in the US that they needed to restructure themselves in order to avoid problems with the Eisenhower administration, the IRS, and the US Department of Justice.[13] According to UCLA scholar Steven Spiegel, opposition from the president was intense:

"The tension between the Eisenhower administration and Israeli supporters was so acute that there were rumors (unfounded as it turned out) that the administration would investigate the American Zionist Council. Therefore, an independent lobbying group was formed within the auspices of the American Zionist Committee." [14]

AIPAC's original internal codename in the American Zionist Committee was "the Kenen Committee." Its results have been unparalleled in the history of foreign lobbying. An AIPAC obituary declared that the State Department strenuously opposed Kenen's earliest lobbying efforts. The indefatigable Kenen worked members of Congress and obtained initial approval of $15 million in aid to Israel, despite robust State Department opposition. This early success set AIPAC's strategy of seeking aid to Israel not on the basis of merit, presidential administration prerogative as the maker of foreign policy, or broad State Department initiatives, but through fake grassroots efforts financed by foreign funds from Israel to "prime the American pump." The Israel lobbying campaign for favorable public relations and media coverage included strategically directed gifts and grants to US colleges and universities for new Israel-centric "Middle East Studies" departments and unfettered lobbying with tax-exempt funds recycled from overseas into the US political system. Activity reports from this intensive campaign are documented in the first chapter.

By 1973, Kenen was able to claim that he had boosted U.S. aid to Israel to $1 billion per year. When Kenen retired in 1974, he still retained his "editor emeritus" title at the *Near East Report*. The spirit of AIPAC's hardball and often illegal tactics would continue long after Kenen left the scene, and the results are staggering. **At the time of Kenen's death in 1988, US aid to Israel exceeded $3 billion a year, the highest amount of US aid given to any country.** [15]

It is popularly believed that the immense power of the Israel lobby sprang from broad grassroots commitment by concerned individuals across America. However, evidence from internal American Zionist Council and AIPAC documents reveals a different history. Many groups, including Christian religious organizations now highly active in AIPAC-directed affairs, were initially indifferent to or even suspicious of Israeli initiatives. It took millions of dollars of Israeli government and overseas funds and decades of effort to create the public relations, lobbying, and political juggernaut that now dominates in America. However, not all Americans welcomed the formation of Israel's lobby.

Founder Si Kenen's startup activities proved to be so brazen that they were put under the microscope of a US Senate committee investigating the activities of non-diplomatic foreign agents in the United States. The investigation was originally focused on Latin America, but was compelled to investigate the Israel lobby being assembled on US soil. The Senate Committee on Foreign Relations dove headlong into questions about whether the American Zionist Council, AIPAC, the Jewish Agency, and Si Kenen were avoiding Foreign Agents Registration Act declarations or filing false ones, acting as unlawful conduits to launder tax-exempt funds, and illegally disseminating Israeli government propaganda in the United States. This investigation, conducted by Senator James William Fulbright, provides the first outside glimpse into the American Zionist Committee, Si Kenen, and AIPAC.

1963: Senator Fulbright Investigates AIPAC

Arkansas Senator James William Fulbright was an internationalist thought leader in the United States Senate. Fulbright's record as a Southern Democrat encompassed staunch multilateralist support for the creation of the United Nations and opposition to Joseph McCarthy's communist witch hunt. Senator McCarthy repeatedly slandered Fulbright with the moniker "Senator Half-bright." Though eminently qualified, Fulbright was ultimately denied consideration for the position of US Secretary of State because of his uncompromising approach to dealing with Israel.

A notable blemish on Fulbright's legacy was his strong support for racial segregation, but the senator is perhaps most remembered among scholarly beneficiaries and American international exchange students for establishing the Fulbright Fellowship scholarship program. Born in Sumner, Missouri, Fulbright earned a science degree from the University of Arkansas in 1925, but became more worldly and appreciative of international education through study at Oxford University's Pembroke College where he was a Rhodes Scholar. Fulbright's understanding of US law and foreign agent registration requirements were anchored in his legal studies; he earned a law degree from George Washington University Law School in 1934. In the same year, he was admitted to the Washington, DC bar and became an attorney in the US Department of Justice anti-trust division. This legal expertise would serve Fulbright well as he sought to understand one of the most complex and opaque chains of interlinked nonprofit corporations ever to be assembled in the United States.

Fulbright was elected to the United States House of Representatives in 1942. He served one term and became a member of the House Foreign Affairs Committee. The House adopted the 1942 Fulbright Resolution, which not only supported the concept of international peacekeeping forces, but also put the United States on track to participate in the League of Nations, which became the United Nations in 1945. In 1944, Fulbright rode a wave of increasing national fame to a Senate seat, and ultimately served five full terms. Fulbright became a member of the Senate Foreign Relations Committee in 1949, and would go on to become the committee's longest-standing chair, serving from 1959 to 1974.

In 1962, Senator Fulbright became concerned about the activities of unregistered foreign agents working to influence public opinion and policy in the United States. His interest was piqued by a pair of articles authored by journalist Walter Pincus and Douglass Cater. Their reporting detailed US-backed Dominican Republic dictator Rafael Trujillo's attempts to use US media for public relations. They also uncovered the Guatemalan regime's covert purchase of friendly coverage in the *American Mercury*, a magazine founded by H.L. Mencken in 1924.[16]

Fulbright offered Walter Pincus a temporary research assignment investigating the scope and breadth of the US activities of unregistered foreign agents. Pincus worked as staff director of the two-member investigatory subcommittee, bringing on staff counsel Charles P. Sifton (now a senior federal judge in Brooklyn).[17] Pincus duly documented Trujillo's efforts to influence Kennedy administration sugar policies and other Latin American foreign agency issues through a series of overseas fact-finding trips. However, the Fulbright hearings were not at all limited to Latin America. They investigated ten lobbying groups suggested by Pincus that paralleled his news reports including China, West Germany, and Ghana.[18] The investigators also subpoenaed documents, developed evidence, and called witnesses from important and highly active Zionist organizations in the United States that were established and given seed money by Israeli-government-related entities. Fulbright focused on the central funding role of the Jewish Agency in Jerusalem and New York, Israeli government propaganda and ownership of the Jewish Telegraphic Agency, and funding for publications including the *Near East Report* and *Israel Digest*. The investigation also studied the conduits and internal financial operations of the American Zionist Council, Si Kenen, and AIPAC.

Fulbright held these 1963 Senate Foreign Relations Committee hearings on foreign agents in a series of closed sessions. The May 23 and August 1 sessions focused entirely on Israel-related operations. Although subsequent news accounts and books would summarize or reference the outcome of the hearings, often with errors or omissions, few ever captured the lengthy, penetrating, and captivating verbal interchanges between Senator Fulbright and witnesses from the organizations subpoenaed to testify. A typical reference to the commission, published in 1970 by a now-defunct Dow Jones weekly newspaper, the *National Observer*, neatly summarized the investigation's outcome:

> In 1963 the Senate Foreign Relations Committee investigated the Jewish Agency and uncovered a "conduit" operation run by an organization called the American Zionist Council. Over an eight-year period, this council received more than $5,000,000 from the Jewish Agency to create a favorable public opinion in this country for Israeli government policies. The Senate investigation closed down the conduit, but the extensive propaganda activities still go on.[19]

Contemporary readers delving into the source material for that article may be astounded by the frank, businesslike proceedings in the transcripts, now released from their dank captivity in federal government archives. Wonderment, confusion, and angst shine through the brilliant exchanges as Fulbright presents subpoenaed evidence, analyzes data, and calls for further information, all while grilling evasive witnesses. Modern-day members of Congress unfamiliar with Fulbright's dialectic will be astonished to see how government oversight and subpoena power functioned in an era when the House and Senate still accommodated leadership capable of challenging issues as sensitive as the US-Israel relationship. Fulbright and the Foreign Relations Committee were ready, willing, and able to compel high-ranking figures within the Israel lobby elite to appear and explain their foreign lobbying and public relations activities.

Senator Fulbright strove to uncover details about myriad indirect payments made by the quasi-governmental Jewish Agency to AIPAC founder Si Kenen and the American Zionist Council. The Jewish Agency was required to file periodic Foreign Agents Registration Act declarations with the US Department of Justice. Fulbright uncovered major covert initiatives designed to influence US policy through media campaigns, indirectly subsidizing lobbyists such as Si Kenen and promoting Israeli government initiatives that were not being disclosed in FARA filings as required by law.

The Jewish Agency: Seed Money from Abroad

The central role of the quasi-governmental Jewish Agency in establishing and funding initiatives through "conduits" resurfaces repeatedly in testimony to Fulbright and the Senate Foreign Relations Committee. Witnesses described the Jewish Agency as an independent organization with national affiliates similar to the International Red Cross.[20] One unknowing conduit of Jewish Agency funds, the Rabinowitz Foundation, described it simply as an agency of the Israeli government, only to later retract the statement under pressure from the Jewish Agency's New York legal counsel. In the following select passages from the May 23, 1960 hearing, witnesses Isadore Hamlin, the executive director of the Jewish Agency-American Section, and the Jewish Agency's legal counsel Maurice M. Boukstein of the New York firm Guzik and Boukstein grapple with Senator Fulbright over the *de facto* status of the Jewish Agency. They also attempt to define the relationship between the Jewish Agency's American subsidiary incorporated in New York under a broad reorganization in 1960 and the executive headquarters in Jerusalem. The Jewish Agency established its first representative office in New York in 1944.[21] Boukstein, in later testimony, would take credit for being one of the legal "architects"[22] of the system of interlocking nonprofit corporations doing end-runs around the clear intent of the Foreign Agents Registration Act.

Testimony would also reveal a direct connection between the nascent lobby and a little-known Israeli false-flag terror attack against the United

States in Eqypt. One board member of the Jewish Agency responsible for "colonization" in Israel and financing the startup of Israel's lobby in America was instrumental in engineering a cover-up of the terror bombing campaign codenamed "Operation Susannah."

Senator Fulbright: The Jewish Agency-American Section, Inc., is, I understand, a New York membership corporation organized in 1960?
Mr. Hamlin: It is, sir.
Senator Fulbright: And since 1960 it has been registered under the Foreign Agents Registration Act of 1938, as amended, as an agent of the Executive of the Jewish Agency for Israel in Jerusalem?
Mr. Hamlin: Mr. Chairman, would you just repeat the date when that filing took place?
Senator Fulbright: 1960.
Mr. Hamlin: 1960: that is correct.
Senator Fulbright: The relationship between the Executive and the American Section, is this contractual or not?
Mr. Hamlin: The American Section is part of the worldwide body called the Jewish Agency Executive. The Jewish Agency Executive is composed of 22 individuals, of which 6 reside in the United States, and so the American Section is part of the worldwide organization.
Mr. Boukstein: May I be of some assistance, Mr. Chairman?
Senator Fulbright: Yes.
Mr. Boukstein: The Executive, as was stated this morning, the Executive of the Jewish Agency is in Jerusalem: the American Section is exactly what it connotes. It is the American Section of the Executive which resides in the United States and functions for and on behalf of the Executive in Jerusalem.
Senator Fulbright: I was trying to clarify the record precisely what the word "Executive" means here. Does it mean the Executive committee of the Jewish Agency?
Mr. Boukstein: It is—do you want me to answer or the witness?
Senator Fulbright: The witness can answer.
Mr. Hamlin: It is in essence the Executive committee.
Senator Fulbright: Of the Jewish Agency?
Mr. Hamlin: Of the Jewish Agency; that is right.
Senator Fulbright: And it is composed of 22 people?
Mr. Hamlin: Pardon me?
Senator Fulbright: Of 22 people?
Mr. Hamlin: Of 22 individuals; yes sir.
Senator Fulbright: And six of those live in the United States?
Mr. Hamlin: Correct, sir.
Senator Fulbright: So that leaves 16 of them who live in Israel?
Mr. Hamlin: That is right, sir.
Senator Fulbright: Now are there any other members? Is this the whole body? Is there a board of directors other than the Executive?

Mr. Hamlin: No, sir. That is the governing body of the Jewish Agency, the total body.

Senator Fulbright: It is a corporation?

Mr. Hamlin: Yes.

Senator Fulbright: Does it have any stockholders?

Mr. Hamlin: No, not to my knowledge.

Senator Fulbright: It is incorporated by a special act of the Government of Israel, is that correct?

Mr. Hamlin: The Jewish Agency, yes, was recognized by special act of the Israeli Parliament.

Senator Fulbright: Are any members of the Executive living in Israel members of the Government?

Mr. Hamlin: Members of our Executive are members of the Government of Israel? Yes, sir.

Senator Fulbright: Who are they?

Mr. Hamlin: One member of our executive, Mr. Eshkol, is a member of the Israeli Government.

Senator Fulbright: What is his position in the Israeli Government?

Hamlin: He is the Minister of Finance. But, if I may add, in the Executive he has competence in one area of work, and that is the area of colonization.

Mr. Boukstein: If I may add, a member of the Executive, Mr. Shazar, was the day before yesterday elected the President of Israel, as you probably noticed in the newspapers.

Senator Fulbright: Does this disqualify him to be a member of the Executive?

Mr. Hamlin: Yes, it would disqualify him.

Senator Fulbright: Could you describe how the Executive—the relationship between the Executive and the American Section, how does the Executive, in other words, exercise control, if it does, over the American Section.

Mr. Hamlin: The American Section is the representative in the United States of the Jerusalem Agency—did you say exercise control, sir?

Senator Fulbright: If it does; yes. Does it exercise control?

Mr. Hamlin: I would say that in the final analysis there would be a vote of all 22 members.

Senator Fulbright: Yes.

Mr. Hamlin: On an issue which might bind them.

Senator Fulbright: Yes.

Mr. Hamlin: But if my experience would indicate anything, I would say that in matters that deal with American affairs, such as we have, the Jerusalem Executive more or less depends on the opinions of their members residing in the United States.

Senator Fulbright: Does this organization have a set of bylaws?

Mr. Hamlin: Yes.

Senator Fulbright: Do we have a copy?

Mr. Sifton: We have, again, an uncertified copy and perhaps, formally, we should have a certified copy.

Mr. Boukstein. Mr. Chairman, we will be glad to furnish it.

Senator Fulbright: He says you will furnish a certified copy of the bylaws of the Executive.

Mr. Hamlin Yes; we would be glad to, sir.

Mr. Boukstein: He will have to certify it as the secretary.

Mr. Fulbright: Yes; that is correct. That is of the Executive. Now, you also have a corporation of the American Section. It is incorporated in this country?

Mr. Hamlin: Yes, sir; New York State.

Senator Fulbright: And you could supply that?

Mr. Boukstein: I think there is a misunderstanding, Mr. Chairman. The Executive of Jerusalem has no bylaws.

Senator Fulbright: Not in Jerusalem?

Mr. Hamlin: I misunderstood you.

Mr. Boukstein. I though you were referring to the bylaws of the American Section and those, of course, we will supply you.

Senator Fulbright: What are the basic guidelines for the Executive in Jerusalem? Under what authority does it operate?

Mr. Hamlin: It is the constitution of the organization.

Senator Fulbright: Does that constitution set out how it should operate?

Mr. Hamlin: Yes. There is a constitution and there are standing rules of the organization.

Senator Fulbright: Could we have those then? Those are the equivalent of the bylaws; that is what I did not know exactly the terminology you used. But you could make that available?

Mr. Hamlin: Yes, sir; I would be glad to.

Senator Fulbright: Do you execute and prepare the registration? [FARA registration]

Mr. Boukstein: Mr. Chairman, as I am the expert on the subject, having acted for the Agency as counsel. The constitution defines the function of the Executive. There is no document that I am aware of that lays down the working rules, such as we would in this country refer to as bylaws of the Executive. They act by resolution.

Senator Fulbright: Well, do they act under majority rule?

Mr. Boukstein. They act under majority rule by resolution.

Senator Fulbright: Do they have subcommittees?

Mr. Boukstein: They have subcommittees which they appoint ad hoc or sometimes continuing subcommittees, Mr. Chairman. But we shall search— but I am aware of the existence of no document which would be the equivalent of rules or bylaws.

Senator Fulbright: Do they have minutes of meetings?

Mr. Boukstein: Yes, they do.

Senator Fulbright: Could you supply us with copies of the minutes of their meetings since 1960?

Mr. Boukstein: Mr. Chairman, I am not so sure that would be a pertinent document. The minutes are in Jerusalem. They relate to all kinds of matters. If you mean excerpts of minutes relating to activities in the United States, we will be glad to furnish them. But I don't think that you have any interest in minutes relating to matters of completely ungermane subjects.

Senator Fulbright: No; we wouldn't request anything ungermane. It was my understanding from testimony this morning that a very large percentage of the funds of the Executive derive from this country, is that correct?

Mr. Boukstein: That is correct.

Senator Fulbright: I will agree that not all of it would be. I was interested in how this Agency operates. I don't know of any precedent of anything like it in any other instance, and I thought it would be interesting to the committee to understand how foreign agents in this particular field operate and what kind of principals they represent.

Mr. Hamlin: Would you like for us to give you a description of the departments and operations in Israel, sir?

Senator Fulbright: Well, if you would care to very briefly.

Mr. Hamlin: All right. Do you want it now?

Senator Fulbright: You can do it in writing.

Mr. Hamlin: Yes sir, we can do it in writing, as you wish.

Senator Fulbright: Are you acquainted with an organization known as the American Zionist Council?

Mr. Hamlin: Yes, sir, I am.

Senator Fulbright: Subsequent to April 1, 1960, did the Jewish Agency-American Section make payments to the American Zionist Council?

Mr. Hamlin: Yes, sir.

Senator Fulbright: To the best of your knowledge, when did these payments begin?

Mr. Hamlin: If my memory serves me, I believe in 1961 for the budget of the Council.

Senator Fulbright: The first of the year, about?

Mr. Hamlin: I would have to look it up.

Senator Fulbright: Would you provide the committee with a record of such payments as you have made to the American Zionist Council?

Mr. Hamlin: Yes, sir, we would.

Senator Fulbright: The American Zionist Council.

Mr. Hamlin: Yes, sir.

Senator Fulbright: In general, what were the purposes of these payments?

Mr. Hamlin: The purposes of these payments were to assist the American Zionist Council carry out its Zionist educational and youth work, and its public informational activities.[23]

Boukstein's efforts to shield "ungermane" offshore operations from Senate scrutiny were purposeful. Even with limited sworn testimony, Fulbright established a direct line of funding flowing from a key government official and an Israeli-government-founded, quasi-governmental entity—the Jewish Agency in Israel—to AIPAC's precursor within several minutes. Fulbright also raised several issues relevant to the Foreign Agents Registration Act. As the recipient of US donations as well as funds from other donor countries, the

Jewish Agency passed funds through the American Section to entities across the United States through the American Zionist Council. Later testimony and subpoenaed documents reveal that the American Zionist Council was washing away the appearance of foreign control in order to finance "policy research" and other public relations activities, as well as fortifying the position and financial muscle of the nascent US-based Israel lobby groups so they could some day take over with no need for further foreign seed or startup funding. Fulbright was right to be concerned about these Jewish Agency operations, for which he did not see "precedent of anything like it in any other instance," as we detail in the final chapter. Decades after Fulbright's investigation, the Jewish Agency and its US partners would be found by Israeli prosecutor Talia Sason to have engaged in laundering $50 billion toward numerous illegal overseas activities.

Although it didn't seem relevant at the time, the Jewish Agency Executive board member who was also minister of finance in the Israeli government serves as the most powerful example of why it was never in America's best interest to have a foreign principal establishing and empowering a stealth lobby in the United States. The minister referred to only by last name with "competence in one area of work, the area of colonization" was Levi Eshkol. At the time of Fulbright's inquiry, Eshkol was ending his 12-year stint as minister of finance and would soon become the ruling Mapai Party leader. When Prime Minister Ben-Gurion resigned in June 1963, Eshkol was elected Mapai party chairman. He was then appointed Prime Minister of Israel. His previously close relationship with Ben-Gurion soon turned hostile over a single matter of burning importance to the United States.

In the summer of 1954, Israel conducted a covert false-flag operation in Egypt known as "Operation Susannah." Israeli agents launched terrorist bombing attacks against US-, British-, and Egyptian-owned targets in Egypt. Since 1950, it had been US policy to pressure the British to withdraw from the Suez Canal and abandon two treaties: the Anglo-Egyptian Treaty of 1936, which made the canal a neutral zone under British control, and the Convention of Constantinople. Israel feared that a British withdrawal would remove a check on Egyptian president Gamal Abdel Nasser's military ambitions. After Israel's diplomatic efforts failed to convince the British to stay, Israel unleashed a false-flag terrorist operation designed to convince the British to stay while framing the Egyptians. Israeli Defense Minister Pinhas Lavon was forced to resign because of the incident, and the scandal came to bear his name. The break between Ben-Gurion and Eshkol occurred over Ben-Gurion's insistence on fully investigating and learning lessons from the sordid Lavon Affair. Eshkol was insistent that investigating the affair was a waste of time, and wished to bury it as soon as possible. On December 13, 1964, he addressed the issue to the Mapai Central Committee.

> "If I vote in favor of an inquiry into the Lavon Affair...We would be opening a Pandora's box of troubles. It will not end with this affair or with this

investigation. We'll be spending the next fifteen years dealing with investigations into various unsolved matters."[24]

Levi Eshkol, the Jewish Agency executive overseeing funding for the establishment of the Israel lobby in the United States, successfully quashed Ben-Gurion's demand to appoint a judicial enquiry into Israel's false-flag attack on America when he became prime minister of Israel.[25]

Jewish Agency Payments to AIPAC's Founder

Senator Fulbright attempted to shine a spotlight on how Si Kenen financed his US lobbying activities through Jewish Agency funding during the hearings. A June 17, 1963 Senate Foreign Relations request for information demanded "year-by-year accounting of the payments made by the Jewish Agency—American Section, Inc. through the American Zionist Council directly to Mr. I.L. Kenen and/or to the American Israel Public Affairs Committee."[26] In a contorted written statement, the Jewish Agency denied making any payments to Kenen. However, subpoenaed evidence outlined how the Agency was, in its words, "making funds available for the Account of the Jewish Agency in the sums listed below." The Jewish Agency explained, "The American Zionist Council had advised the Jewish Agency—American Section Inc. that it needed these funds in order that it might pay the same on account of its indebtedness to the *Near East Report*, a publication issued in Washington, D.C. by Mr. I. L. Kenen in his private capacity." [27] Between June 29, 1960 and October 13, 1961, Kenen received $38,000, mainly in $5,000 increments, from the Jewish Agency through the American Zionist Council. [28]

Senator Fulbright expressed confusion over Kenen's remuneration and a wide-ranging dialogue over how US organizations acted as conduits for the Jewish Agency and subsidized subscriptions to the *Near East Report* ensued. Fulbright again grilled two witnesses: the Jewish Agency's American Section executive director Isadore Hamlin and his legal counsel, Maurice M. Boukstein of the New York firm Guzik and Boukstein.[29] They also discussed the reorganization of Jewish Agency operations in the United States and why AIPAC founder Si Kenen was no longer registered as a foreign agent of Israel.

Senator Fulbright: Honestly, Mr. Hamlin, I find it extremely difficult to follow this, and I am reading it so I hope you will clarify it....there then follows seven separate $5,000 payments amounting—with one $3,000—amounting to $38,000. I won't read all of them. I would like to ask you, why did you not pay the $38,000 directly to Mr. Kenen? Why do you go through all this rigmarole? Mr. Hamlin: Sir, the answer is we would have no reason to pay this money directly to Mr. Kenen. The money was for the specific purposes of buying subscriptions for a list of the American Zionist Council.

Senator Fulbright: I don't understand this language here. What you mean is you just paid it to the Zionist Council, is that right?

Mr. Hamlin: We would have normally paid the American Zionist Council; yes, as we did in previous periods.

Senator Fulbright: But you knew it was for the purpose of paying Mr. Kenen.

Mr. Hamlin: Yes, sir.

Senator Fulbright: Were these actually for subscription—

Mr. Hamlin: If I may correct that, so that the record will be absolutely clear, this was payment to the American Zionist Council so that the American Zionist Council could straighten out their affairs with Mr. Kenen in connection with the subscription.

Senator Fulbright: If you can make this record clear, you are a genius far beyond anyone I have ever met anywhere.

Mr. Hamlin: I am sorry.

Senator Fulbright: It is not clear to me what you gain by all this rigmarole. Why didn't you pay Mr. Kenen directly? He was serving your purpose, wasn't he?

1958 $20,000 Payment from the Jewish Agency to the American Zionist Council[30]

(Source: Subpoenaed Documents, Fulbright Hearing)

Mr. Hamlin: Mr. Kenen had no connection with us whatsoever. I stress again, Mr. Chairman, the American Zionist Council appealed to the American Section, to the Jewish Agency-American Section, to grant a certain amount of money, and this has been going on for several years so that the American

Zionist Council could get the *Near East Report* mailed to a large mailing list in which the American Zionist Council was interested. Therefore—

Senator Fulbright: You were interested, too, weren't you?

Mr. Hamlin: This was within our general purpose certainly.

Senator Fulbright: Of course it was.

Mr. Hamlin: Pardon me.

Senator Fulbright: I say, of course it was. I mean they were serving your purpose, they were all serving your purpose, you had a common purpose with all of them, didn't you, and you had the money.

Mr. Hamlin: Pardon me, sir.

Senator Fulbright: And you had the money.

Mr. Hamlin: Yes, sir; we did. Fortunately.

Senator Fulbright: Who owns the building at 515 Park Avenue?

Mr. Hamlin: The building at 515 Park Avenue is at this time owned by the Jewish Agency for Israel, Inc.

Senator Fulbright: At this time, when—has it changed recently or how long have you owned it?

Mr. Hamlin: It was always owned by the Jewish Agency, Inc.

Mr. Boukstein: He hopes to own it.

Senator Fulbright: About the payment to Mr. Kenen, were these actually for subscriptions?

Mr. Hamlin: Sir, the American Zionist Council came to us and said, "Please let us have an appropriation of funds so that we could straighten out our affairs in connection with the subscription list that we gave Mr. Kenen for distribution of the *Near East Report.*

Senator Fulbright: Well, I have a letter from Mr. Kenen, a sworn letter, on the 31st of July, 1963—that was yesterday. It says:

(READS ALOUD LETTER)

1963 Kenen Letter About the Near East Report

(Source: Fulbright Hearing[31])

Washington, D.C., July 31, 1963

Dear Senator Fulbright:

Thank you for the opportunity to read and comment on testimony taken by the Senate Committee on Foreign Relations on May 23.

I wish to refer specifically to statements which appear on pages 1252 and 1253 and which suggest that I received $20,000 per year from the American Zionist Council for personal services.

The fact is that I was paid a fee of $100 per week for my personal services, consisting mainly of speaking engagements—about one a week—before national and local bodies of the American Zionist Council, its constituent organizations, and other groups throughout the United States. The balance received from the American Zionist Council was in payments for subscriptions to the *Near East Report*, which I publish and edit, and in reimbursement for travel, printing, and office expenses. My personal services to the council ended July 1, 1960.

The *Near East Report*, established in 1957, is sold on a subscription basis to many organizations and individuals throughout the United States. The American Zionist Council purchased subscriptions for its leaders and regional offices, for newspaper editors and educators. These subscriptions, averaging about 23 percent of the total circulation, expired in 1962.

Very truly,

I.L. Kenen

Senator Fulbright: Here I would gather he says he is an employee, or was, of the American Zionist Council; he is not an independent entrepreneur the way you described a moment ago, according to his letter.

Mr. Hamlin: Sir, I don't know the relationship between Mr. Kenen and the American Zionist Council. But the letter is clear, that he performed certain services to the American Zionist Council. Now, what we are discussing is my answer to this question is a subsequent period to this relationship and refers only to subscriptions to the *Near East Report*

Senator Fulbright: Well now, this change in status came about approximately the same time as you reorganized your whole operation in America, did it not?

Mr. Hamlin: Yes, it did.

Senator Fulbright: Now, was this change of Mr. Kenen's status part of the reorganization, so instead of paying him directly, you now buy enough subscriptions to pay him?

Mr. Hamlin: It would not, sir.

Senator Fulbright: Why not? Doesn't he perform very much the same function as he did before? He serves the same purpose.

Mr. Hamlin: No, sir, not at all.

Senator Fulbright: Why not?

Mr. Hamlin: He was performing speaking services during that earlier period. We were giving the American Zionist Council a money grant for subscriptions for the *Near East Report*

Senator Fulbright: Doesn't he speak anymore?

Mr. Hamlin: To my knowledge, he has no connection now, no arrangements with, the Zionist Council.

Senator Fulbright: But he writes these letters, doesn't he?

Mr. Hamlin: Pardon me?

Senator Fulbright: He writes the *Near East Report*

Mr. Hamlin: Yes, sir, he does.

Senator Fulbright: And he sends them to all sorts of people free of charge, doesn't he?

Mr. Hamlin: I am sorry, sir?

Senator Fulbright: He sends them all around free of charge.

Mr. Hamlin: Free of charge? I don't know.

Senator Fulbright: Well, you pay for them. I mean the arrangement is that you, through the Council, pay for them and they send them to a list who do not subscribe, is this not correct? I can see from my own experience. He sends me one, and I don't pay for it.

Mr. Hamlin: Sir, the Council provided the funds—

Senator Fulbright: Is it me or the committee? Maybe I do him an injustice but we get one; maybe it is the committee.

Mr. Boukstein: Mr. Chairman, it is obvious from what the witness said that a large number of recipients of the bulletins don't pay for it.

Senator Fulbright: That is right.

Mr. Boukstein: The American Zionist Council pays for a number of them.

Senator Fulbright: That is right.

Mr. Boukstein: But nevertheless, the impression should not be left that that is the bulk of the majority or the major part of the recipients of the publication. My information is that it isn't so, and while you permit me, Mr. Chairman—

Senator Fulbright: I missed that, wait a minute. What is not so?

Mr. Boukstein: That the number of people receiving—that the people receiving bulletins are—what is it called, the *Near East Report*—which are paid for by the American Zionist Council, are not the majority of recipients. I don't know the exact percentage, but it is only a part of the number published and distributed. Now, while I am at it, Mr. Chairman, I would like to say one more word so that you will have the information.

I personally in my capacity as counsel had a great deal to do with the reorganization which took place in 1960. I participated in many meetings. At no time, Mr. Chairman, did the services or functions of Mr. Kenen enter into a discussion which had anything to do with the reorganization or the purposes for the reorganization. I am saying this simply so that the record be clear and so that no unfair inferences may be drawn as to the payments being made to Mr. Kenen.

Senator Fulbright: I am reminded, Mr. Kenen in his own letter says that these subscriptions, from the Zionist Council, average about 23 percent of the total circulation expired in 1962. You do not regard Mr. Kenen, for practical purposes, as an employee of the Agency?

Mr. Hamlin: Definitely not.

Senator Fulbright: Do you find his policies in disagreement with yours?

Mr. Hamlin: I know Mr. Kenen as a director of the American Israel Public Affairs Committee, which is composed of distinguished citizens of this country. He travels around, they have a fundraising campaign. These are not tax–exempt funds which Mr. Kenen carries on his activities as a director of that committee.

Senator Fulbright: What are his activities in Washington? Are you familiar with it?

Mr. Hamlin: Not in detail, no, sir. But he is a registered lobbyist in Washington in his capacity as a director of the American Israel Public Affairs Committee.

Senator Fulbright: He is a registered lobbyist under the domestic lobbying law?

Mr. Hamlin: That is right, sir.

Senator Fulbright: Why do you think he shouldn't register under the Foreign Agents Registration Act?

Mr. Hamlin: Excuse me. I can't comment on that, Mr. Chairman.

Mr. Boukstein: I am not acting here for Mr. Kenen, Mr. Chairman.

Senator Fulbright: Well, maybe we ought to ask Mr. Kenen. Do you think he would be competent to answer that question?

Mr. Boukstein: I assume he would be. My offhand opinion would be that he does not have to register under the Foreign Agents Act, not from the facts as disclosed in this, in the executive session, or at this hearing.

Senator Fulbright: Not as disclosed, but from the facts as you know them?

Mr. Boukstein: Let me go further. From the facts as I know them, he would not have to register.

Senator Fulbright: Mr. Boukstein, I would not hesitate to challenge your opinion about whether he should register or not, but for the life of me I can't understand why a person who received such a large subsidy from a foreign agent indirectly, because it goes through the American Zionist Council, should not have to register, whereas if he received it directly, I think you would agree he would have to register, wouldn't he?

Mr. Boukstein: He—

Senator Fulbright: And the device of merely using the American Zionist Council seems to me to be a very thin way of insulating him from the effects of the Foreign Registration Act.

Mr. Boukstein: Mr. Chairman, he is selling a service, he is publishing a bulletin. If there are any debts or any liabilities, he or his corporation are responsible for them. As a matter of fact, when the American Zionist Council ceased paying him for the bulletin, he ceased sending out copies to the list which they had furnished him. I don't believe he is subject to registration under those conditions.

Senator Fulbright: I have seen a number of his publications, and if they aren't completely devoted to the promotion of the purposes of your—the same purposes, the Jewish Agency, and the state of Israel, I don't know what is. It is directed to that purpose. I am not criticizing the purpose. You have a right to do it. You do it, and you register for it. I just am not quite clear why Mr. Kenen, who serves the same purpose, and, in fact, in some ways much more directly in his contact with Congress than you are, why he shouldn't have to register?

Mr. Boukstein: Mr. Chairman, this is not the only publication which is favorable to Israel in the United States; there are others.

Senator Fulbright: I have no doubt of it. Certainly, the *New York Times*, the *Washington Post*, I could name a hundred of them, I guess, they are very favorable and I am not suggesting they are in your employ. I am suggesting that Mr. Kenen is receiving far more of his funds from the Jewish—the Israel

Government directly and indirectly than is the *New York Times*. They are doing it strictly on their own, at least as far as I know.

Senator Fulbright (continued): I really shouldn't speak authoritatively because we haven't looked at it, but it is quite clear Mr. Kenen has been, for practical purposes, as he states himself, up to a certain point of your reorganization, he was on your payroll. Then, in order to insulate him, you took this indirect way of paying him by buying his product and paying him in that way. I am only trying to understand how this is done. I don't know why he shouldn't register.[32]

Senator Fulbright had uncovered one subterfuge of the 1960 reorganization that, with the perspective of 40 years, we can now examine with cross-references to data from current AIPAC operations. The *Near East Report* was never a commercially viable subscription-based publication. Rather than true subscriptions received from readers, it was subsidized with funds that came mostly from Israel via the Jewish Agency. When the newsletter was a startup,. Si Kenen was essentially receiving a hidden foreign subsidy for his lobbying activities within *Near East Report* publication revenues. If the newsletter was structured then as it is currently, nearly 21% of total revenues generated would have been available to Si Kenen alone, not counting extra gross margin for office space, travel, and other overhead. The *Near East Report's* last filed tax return (Near East Research, Inc.) indicates that in the year 2005, $154,212 (21% of the total revenue of $736,855)[33] went to the publication's director. If Kenen ran the *Near East Report* the way it is currently run, he could have also subsidized his lobbying travel with 11% of the newsletter's gross revenue (at $79,801 currently). Today, AIPAC raises funds for the *Near East Report* with no pretense that those who run it are, as Boukstein asserted, "selling a service" or financing it with what commercially viable magazine and newspaper publishers would call "subscriptions."

Although the Jewish Agency and American Zionist Council would continue to claim an arms-length subscription relationship with Si Kenen, their own internal notes revealed that the payments were meant for Kenen.

Senator Fulbright: Well, I now show you an undated handwritten note and signed "OK. I. Hamlin," and ask you if you signed and approved the payment set forth in this note?

Mr. Hamlin: Yes, sir. This is my signature.

Senator Fulbright: The main part of the note deals with "HK Subventions," but I call your attention to the line reading "Kenen (paid 1/14 5,000)" which has a line drawn through it and the initials "OK" next to it, and ask you if this refers to I.L. Kenen?

Mr. Hamlin: Sir, I will have to look, try to find out what happened in this case. But it is possible that when we made the payments to the Council for Kenen we may have, that is, for the purpose of these subscriptions of the *Near East Report*, which was done by the American Zionist Council, for the sake of bookkeeping, for the sake of our internal records, it may have been designated as "Kenen," just as in the case of these memorandums I designated "Shwadran" just to save time.

Senator Fulbright: I am just trying to clarify the record on this. Could you file for the record the payments that you made through the American Zionist council to Mr. Kenen?[34]

Kenen's lobbying was not the only activity financed by Israel through the Jewish Agency. During the course of the May 23, 1963 hearing, Fulbright presented and placed into the record field reports discussed at Jewish Agency and American Zionist Council meetings about the success of Israeli government propaganda media placements. On October 23, 1962, Mrs. Judith Epstein, chair of the American Zionist Council's Department of Information, filed a field report about the department's accomplishments. Her budget had fallen from $750,000 to $175,500 since part of the work of the American Zionist Council had, in her words, "now been taken over by the Kenen Committee, which was charged with political action, formerly in the province of the American Zionist Council. All approaches on the Hill to the political parties, etc. are now the responsibility of the American Israel Public Affairs Committee whose funds are not tax-exempt. Thus the greater emphasis is now put on the more subtle approach, which, through positive presentation of Israel's accomplishments, aims and purpose, and by counterattack of the many enemies of Israel and the Zionist movement..."[35]

Epstein mentioned efforts of the American Zionist Council's Information Department toward preparing responses to what they considered hostile reports appearing in such hotbeds of anti-Israel foment as *Cosmopolitan, The Columbia University Quarterly Forum,* and *Editor and Publisher.* These were among "25 responses to newspapers or magazines that are written or sent" in an average month.[36] The American Zionist Council was "following closely" the "Arab States with their numerous embassies and consulates, the Arab Information Office, the American Friends of the Middle East, and the American Council of Judaism", but urged that "local Councils be strengthened throughout the country so that we may be kept informed of anti-Israel activities..."[37] The Middle East Institute in Washington, DC was also being closely watched for "anti-Israel propaganda of a subtle nature."[38] The department formed a campus watch group called the Inter-University Committee on Israel, which expanded from its base in New York to place favorable articles in "leading academic publications" in the US. [39]

The American Zionist Council also established a "Magazine Committee" chaired by a "man who holds a key position on the editorial level in the magazine business. He knows everyone in the trade, has important contacts and exploits them on behalf of Israel." [40] This unnamed editor led a committee composed of "15 writers and editors who are eminent in their respective fields" that has "built up a 'bank of ideas' for freelance writers who go to Israel in search of articles and has provided the Israelis with a better idea of the kind of material which is acceptable to the American reading public and magazine editors. We cannot pinpoint all that has already been accomplished by this committee except to say that it has been responsible for the writing and placement of articles on Israel in some of America's leading magazines."[41] For broadcast media placements, the "TV-Radio Committee" had secured the services of "the director of creative projects of an important TV chain" to arrange for "talks and interviews on radio and TV; submits ideas for possible programs to stations and networks so as to give a better and more sympathetic understanding of Israel to the viewing American public; and takes steps to counteract hostile propaganda in these media. In view of the many millions of Americans who daily watch TV and radio, this is one of the more important media in which we must expand our work."[42]

The Department of Information Speakers Bureau did 2,240 engagements in 1961 with an "absurdly small staff." Targeting multiple community venues, one speaker in a single day would speak at four to seven appearances: "a Rotary Club, a World Affairs Council, a church group, a high school assembly or college group, a woman's club, a TV or Radio appearance, a background session with a local editor or commentator, etc." with the majority of "engagements before non-Jewish groups."[43]

According to the field report, the American Zionist Council Research Bureau "analyzes books and articles that deal with Israel or the Middle East. When a book is favorable, it is recommended. When it is unfavorable, it is analyzed and distortions are pointed up by providing the factual data required, so that our local councils will be prepared to react to the impact which these books have on the communities."[44]

The Research Bureau also interjected itself into high school textbook content: "The Inter-University Committee has been preparing textbook material as a guide to social science teachers in the junior and senior high schools on the subject of Israel. It would be impossible for these busy academicians to do the painstaking research required..."[45] The Research Bureau also developed centralized policy positions, now commonly referred to as talking points for "informing local Zionist Council leaders and Jewish community leadership as to our recommended position and steps for action on issues such as the Arab refugee problem, the Soblen case,[46] the Jordan water dispute, etc. Similarly we distribute material and advisories for special occasions such as the celebration of Israel's Anniversary, the tenth anniversary of Weizmann's passing, etc."[47]

The American Zionist Council in New York was quick to put out memos and templates for stories to be submitted to local newspapers from local councils across the United States. Propaganda quality control was a key concern. A February 27, 1963 American Zionist Committee memo from Harry A. Steinberg urged that "enclosed herewith suggested material which can be used by you in preparing replies to the Max Freedman articles, in the event they have appeared in one of your local papers. It is not necessary to use all of this material in your own letters to the editor. Use the portions which you feel will make the most impact on your editor and the readership of the paper. We request also that you do not use this material in the submitted form, but that you rewrite it so that letters submitted in various parts of the country do not appear to be identical..."[48] Influencing Christian religious groups was also a key objective of the American Zionist Council.

The American Zionist Council's Commission on Inter-Religious Affairs was responsible for the "effort in gaining friends in the Protestant and Catholic religious communities." In addition to bringing together Orthodox, Conservative, and Reform rabbis, the committee concerned itself with "monitoring the Christian church press, stimulating articles presenting Israeli and Zionist ideology, and answering the hostile attacks very often found in the publications of the Protestant and Catholic Church, as well as cultivating key religious leaders and editors."[49]

The commission held seminars that in Boston alone, attracted 50 Catholic priests, and documented the successful seminar approach in a "Manual for Rabbis giving the know-how of establishing these seminars, steps to be taken and the scope of the subject matter, approach, etc." The commission's work was seen as one of the "great possibilities for the future since one cannot underestimate the impact of public opinion of churchmen in this country."[50] The successful fusion of the power of evangelical Christian groups with the Israel lobby a generation later would prove this analysis to be entirely correct.

The American Zionist Council's Public Relations Advisory Board was reported by Mrs. Epstein to be "our newest Committee which has only had its first meeting, and, therefore, it is difficult to know how it will develop. One of the more important public relations men in this city was invited by the Government of Israel to introduce a course on public relations at the University of Tel Aviv and to help the Government map out better procedures for its own public relations effort. Israel was delighted with the contribution which this man made, and he, in turn, came back excited and deeply interested in Israel and everything for which it stood. We were asked to approach him to build up a committee of public relations men who could be called on when and if problems arose which needed the technical know-how and assistance which only such people could give. Mrs. Epstein approached him, found him most responsive. He sent out a letter and last week 15 of the outstanding public relations men of this city sat around this table to consider how they could be of help in presenting a positive picture of Israel in the U.S."[51]

The range of Department of Information activities described in the American Zionist Council field report, and the fact that they were being financed with Jewish Agency funds, raised Senator Fulbright's ire. The central role of Si Kenen, who had been previously portrayed as a private newsletter editor, in actively lobbying in the US with Jewish Agency funds before the reorganization drew evasive answers from Isadore Hamlin.

Senator Fulbright: Now, let us see. Was this report furnished to the Jewish Agency-American Section by the American Zionist Council?
Mr. Hamlin: Sir, this handwriting on this memorandum indicates to me that it was sent to one of the members of our Executive, who is a member of one of

the governing boards of the American Zionist Council. It happens to be a member of one of the governing boards of the American Zionist Council.

Senator Fulbright: But he is also a member of the Jewish Agency?

Mr. Hamlin: Yes.

Senator Fulbright: Does this report accurately describe the type of activities of the American Zionist Council which were being financed by the Jewish Agency-American Section?

Mr. Hamlin: I cannot answer that question honestly, sir, I do not know.

Senator Fulbright: Who would know about that?

Mr. Hamlin: Sir?

Senator Fulbright: Who would know about that?

Mr. Hamlin: I presume the staff members of the American Zionist Council.

Senator Fulbright: You are not very familiar with what the American Zionist Council does?

Mr. Hamlin: I am in a general way, but I am not an officer there, or an employee, so I cannot vouch for these activities.

Senator Fulbright: Do you approve of the budget that they submit to you?

Mr. Hamlin: No, sir.

Senator Fulbright: Who does?

Mr. Hamlin: The treasurer did in this period.

Senator Fulbright: Who is the treasurer?

Mr. Hamlin: Mr. Louis A. Pincus.

Mr. Boukstein: Mr. Chairman, I think there was a misunderstanding. You did not mean him personally. You mean "you" in the sense of the organization?

Senator Fulbright: Yes, the Jewish Agency.

Mr. Boukstein: He took it to mean, does he personally approve the budget.

Mr. Hamlin: Yes, I did.

Senator Fulbright: Does the Agency approve the budget?

Mr. Hamlin: Yes, sir.

Senator Fulbright: This was a period in 1962 in which, as you have testified before, the Agency is contributing approximately 80 percent of their budget, and it would be quite natural that you would examine and approve or criticize, or what you like, the budget, would it not? I mean not you, in every instance, but I mean the Agency.

Mr. Hamlin: Yes, the organization, certainly. Now, the treasurer of the Jewish Agency was requested by the Executive to negotiate this allocation.

Senator Fulbright: Who did he negotiate with?

Mr. Hamlin: With Rabbi Miller and Mr. Bick, the treasurer of the Council.

Senator Fulbright: That is right.

Mr. Hamlin: Yes, sir.

Senator Fulbright: Take the second paragraph of that memorandum, the report, I guess you would call it. I quote, "At that time the department had a budget of $750,000." What is "the department"?

Mr. Hamlin: Did you ask at what time?

Senator Fulbright: What does "the department" mean?

Mr. Hamlin: The Department of Information.

Senator Fulbright: Department of Information?

Mr. Hamlin: Yes.

Senator Fulbright: (reading) "Today the budget is $175,450 with an obligation to carry on a comprehensive, diverse and complex project which demands personnel and funds. However, she pointed out that the part of the work of the original council had now been taken over by the Kenen Committee, which was charged with political action, formerly in the province of the American Zionist Council. All approaches on the Hill to the political parties, etc. are now the responsibility of the American Israel Public Affairs Committee whose funds are not tax-exempt. Thus the greater emphasis is now put on the more subtle approach, which, through positive presentation of Israel's accomplishments, aims and purpose, and by counterattack of the many enemies of Israel and the Zionist movement."

Was direct political action of the unsubtle type at one time in the province of the American Zionist Council?

Mr. Hamlin: I have no personal knowledge of this, Senator.

Senator Fulbright: What do you mean by the "Kenen Committee"? I have not heard it referred to as a committee before.

Mr. Hamlin: The "Kenen Committee" is the American-Israel Public Affairs Committee.

Senator Fulbright: I thought he was known as some kind of reporter up to now. What did he—

Mr. Boukstein: It was brought out, Senator, he was in two capacities. He is the owner and publisher of a—what is it called—"*Near East Report*." But in addition, he is also the director of the American-Israel Public Affairs Committee.

Senator Fulbright: And that is what this is?

Mr. Boukstein. Yes.

Senator Fulbright: Well, we will just place the report in the record.[52]

The documents that Fulbright placed into the Senate record reveal that $574,550 (the former Department of Information budget of $750,000 minus the then-current budget of $175,450) mysteriously disappeared from the budget around the same time that the "Kenen Committee" or AIPAC was formed. The Jewish Agency's legal counsel refused to affirm what was obvious to Fulbright and the Senate Foreign Relations Committee. The earlier Israel lobbying with tax-exempt funds laundered from overseas was viewed as untenable after the meeting with Fred Scribner, and new artifices were erected to hide activities while continuing the effort. We can surmise from the budget that the formation of AIPAC was an effort that temporarily sapped the "Department of Information" as startup costs were channeled to Kenen and his activities through various hidden conduits. These complex multiple "capacities" of Israel lobby actors such as Kenen again surface in the examination of the activities of other AIPAC leaders. Kenen's multiple roles in lobbying, media, and political and charitable fundraising would be mirrored in the actions of AIPAC's leadership and activists, leading to frequent brushes with the law while necessitating AIPAC's code of total operational secrecy.

American Zionist Committee Funding from the Jewish Agency

The second day of the Senate committee's inquiry into Israeli activities in the United States began with the Jewish Agency's legal counsel attempting to positively frame its activities. Committee Chair Senator Fulbright refocused the session by stressing why so much attention was being focused on the Jewish Agency and the funds it provided to AIPAC's precursor, the American Zionist Council, and both organizations' director, Si Kenen. Fulbright estimated that Israel had spent over $5 million on lobbying and public relations in the US through its foreign agents under investigation. The modern-day equivalent, adjusted for inflation, is over $33 million.

Senator Fulbright: For almost 20 years, the representative of the Jewish Agency has been registered with the Department of Justice, but it was only within the last year, when this committee called attention to the matter, that the registrant was requested by the Department's Registration Section to itemize its two large items of expenditures within the United States: namely, its "Grants and subventions" and its "Payments to affiliates."

As the record of the committee's May 23 hearing shows, the Jewish Agency from January 1, 1955 through December 31, 1962 made payments totaling $5,100,001.02 to the American Zionist Council to carry on activities in the United States.

As Mr. Hamlin has testified previously, the Jewish Agency provided about 80 percent of the American Zionist Council's funds and at the same time used the Council as a conduit for Agency funds destined for other groups, organizations, or individuals.

These payments, prior to October of last year, were lumped together under the two headings mentioned above.

Through its failure to require itemization, the Department of Justice, and, therefore, the public, was unaware of the public relations activities in the interest of Israel carried on within the United States by the Agency. And the Jewish Agency supported organizations and individuals without itemization of such financial support publicly in its Justice Department reports.[53]

After putting into the record a lengthy statement from witness Isadore Hamlin of the Jewish Agency about refugee resettlement activities in Israel, Fulbright cut short the presentation and refocused on the foreign agent question. He also examined Israel-generated domestic policy opposition within the US on an entirely different refugee matter—that of Palestinian refugees.

Senator Fulbright: Your statement is a very good statement, but is quite irrelevant to the subject matter that we are investigating here.

As one example that comes to mind, I believe, is it not a fact that the Zionist Council, which you supported, did vigorously oppose the Johnson report with regard to resettlement of the Arab refugees and solicited opposition to that in the United States?

Mr. Hamlin: I am not thoroughly acquainted with the operations of the American Zionist Council. I am not a member of their governing body nor am I a member of their staff, and so I don't think I could give you any comment on that question.

Senator Fulbright: I was thinking of the memorandum on page 135 of the record of Part 9, which is a memorandum that came from your files.

Mr. Hamlin: Yes, sir, I read that memorandum.

Senator Fulbright: Well, the point is, your Agency supports the American Zionist Council, doesn't it?

Mr. Hamlin: It does, indeed.

Senator Fulbright: It is one of your affiliates. Don't you consider you have some responsibility for what it does?

Mr. Hamlin: Sir, the American Zionist Council is managed by an independent group of distinguished US citizens representing all the Zionist movements in this country.

Senator Fulbright: It isn't financially independent because you support it.

Mr. Hamlin: Beg pardon?

Senator Fulbright: You support it, don't you?

Mr. Hamlin: Yes, sir, we do.

Senator Fulbright: How independent is a matter of opinion, isn't it?[54]

This short exchange about the Johnson report only touches on how Israel could covertly intervene in a US administration's official US Middle East policy through its American lobby. The Kennedy administration aspired to resolve the Palestine refugee problem in 1961-62 through development of a plan for compensation, resettlement, or repatriation under the formal auspices of the United Nations Palestine Conciliation Commission. On August 21, 1961, the US decided to appoint Joseph E. Johnson as its special representative at the United Nations. His task was to visit the Middle East and meet with the regional governments and Israel to explore means of resolving the problem created by the expulsion of Palestine Arab refugees from the newly created state of Israel. Initially, Dr. Johnson was hopeful that it might be possible to take practical steps toward resolving the issue.[55] A key innovation of the plan was free choice for Palestinian refugees: they could choose resettlement in a host Arab country along with compensation for lost property in what was now Israel, or choose to return to homes and properties now in Israel, with no limits on the number making this choice. The negotiations were ultimately torpedoed, and efforts to implement the plan were canceled by the administration in December 1962. A secret but now declassified US State Department memo laid the blame squarely on the efforts of lobby groups

organized and financed by Israel to discredit and destroy the plan without it
appearing to be the work of the government of Israel.

> We consider that Israel, undesirous of repatriating any
> refugees and having finally been persuaded of a serious
> US intent to seek implementation of the Johnson Plan, is
> making an all-out effort to scuttle the plan while the US is
> still not fully committed to it and while there is a
> possibility that the scuttling can be accomplished without
> public onus for Israel. We believe that Israel is charging
> bad faith and is interpreting the language of the plan and
> the explanation in the blackest light as pretexts useful to
> achievement of its objective rather than as causes. If the
> Israelis were sincere they would be willing to engage in
> serious talk with Dr. Johnson. Perhaps having now
> received assurance of the Hawk missile the Israelis feel
> free to take a hard line in the hope of obtaining more
> benefits in the pre-election period. At least one leak on
> the Johnson Plan has appeared in the Israeli press with an
> expression of hostility to it.[56]

Fulbright would also undercut the charade of any "arm's length"
relationship between the Jewish Agency in Israel and the American Zionist
Council when he presented subpoenaed documents revealing a direct
relationship in core financial matters. Contradicting his earlier testimony that
the newly created American Section of the Jewish Agency handled conduit
payments to the American Zionist Council, Isadore Hamlin was forced to
admit to direct financing negotiations between the Jewish Agency in Jerusalem
and the American Zionist Council.

Senator Fulbright: I note that item 10 supplied by you to the committee in
answer to a request for written agreement between the Agency and the
American Zionist Council is a memorandum dated July 10, 1962, which also is
already part of the record.
Is it correct to infer from this agreement that the Zionist Council financing
came directly from the Jerusalem Agency rather than by way of the American
Section? That is on page 1420, I believe.
Mr. Hamlin: Yes, sir, I have that before me.

Jewish Agency funds American Zionist Council

(Source: 1963 Fulbright Hearing[57])

MAY 30, 1962.

Miss FANNIE SPEISER,
Dr. I. MOYAL.

Allocation by the Jewish Agency to AZC for period April 1, 1962 to March 31, 1963.

At a meeting held on June 25, 1962, in which Mr. Pincus, Mr. Bick, Rabbi Unger, and I participated, it was decided:

1. The allocation to the AZC amounting to $712,000 would be paid as follows:

Estimated rent for space occupied by the AZC at 515 Park Ave. (final figure to be agreed upon by Bick, Hamlin, and myself)	$85,000
Estimated service charges (final figure to be adjusted in accordance with actual services rendered)	68,000
Cash payments:	
(a) 4 weekly payments during April 1962, of $14,000 each and 1 lump-sum payment of $10,000	66,000
(b) 4 weekly payments during May 1962, of $16,000 each	64,000
(c) 5 weekly payments during June 1962, of $15,000 each	75,000
(d) 13 weekly payments during July, August, and September 1962, of $12,000 each	156,000
(e) 16 weekly payments of $8,000 and 10 weekly payments of $7,000 each during the period October 1962 to March 1963	198,000
Total	712,000

2. Mr. Bick informed us that he erred when he estimated the amounts due to the Youth Movements for the budgetary year 1961–62 as being $50,000. Bick said that the total amount was actually $60,000. As we have already paid the $50,000, it was agreed that the remaining $10,000 should be divided equally between the AZC and the Jewish Agency. Hence, over and above the amount of $712,000 allocated we shall, at the request of Mr. Bick, pay him the further sum of $5,000.

3. It was further agreed that the $100,000 loan taken by the AZC from Bank Leumi should be the responsibility of the Jewish Agency, although left on the books of the AZC as their debt.

This means that we shall have to pay interest on the note signed by the AZC and guaranteed by us. When the time comes we shall, of course, have to pay the principal.

Senator Fulbright: Is it correct to infer from this memorandum, as it reads here, that the financial arrangements for the Zionist Council were directly with the Jerusalem Agency?

Mr. Hamlin: The Treasurer of the Jewish Agency, Mr. Pincus, negotiated this understanding with the American Zionist Council. Yes, sir.

Senator Fulbright: We will put that item into the record. It is in the record already. On page 1413 of the printed hearings, part 9, among excerpts of Jerusalem Agency minutes supplied this committee by you there is the following:

Publications and Fundraising Budget: American Zionist Council and the Jewish Agency, Israel

(Source: 1963 Fulbright Hearing[58])

> Excerpt from minutes of plenary session of Jewish Agency Executive, Jerusalem, dated June 13, 1960:
> "Allocations to publications of Zionist groups in the United States—it was decided that the sum that was granted to such publications last year—$62,000—from the budget of the Jewish Agency will be granted this year. The Jewish Agency Executive, New York, is asked to find a way of including this sum in the budget of the American Zionist Council."

Senator Fulbright: Did you, in fact, place this sum within the American Zionist Council budget?

Mr. Hamlin: We had a separate budgetary allocation for these payments.

Senator Fulbright: For what?

Mr. Hamlin: We had a separate budgetary allocation for these payments to Zionist groups.

Mr. Fulbright: And did the $62,000, was it placed in their budget, was it paid to them?

Mr. Hamlin: No. It was not placed in the budget of the American Zionist Council, but the funds were remitted to the Zionist groups through the American Zionist Council.

What this statement means, Mr. Chairman, is that it was our hope, it was the hope of the Jewish Agency Executive, that eventually the Zionist groups composing the American Zionist Council, that is, the Council itself, would succeed in developing their own fundraising in the United States, so that eventually this obligation would be taken over by the Council itself. That is the meaning of the wording of this decision.

Senator Fulbright: Well, can you say whether the $62,000 was paid?

Mr. Hamlin: Would you repeat that question?

Senator Fulbright: Was the $62,000 paid?

Mr. Hamlin: Yes, it was paid.

Senator Fulbright: What was that used for by the Zionist Council?

Mr. Hamlin: The Zionist Council did not use the $62,000. The Zionist Council passed this money or made this money available to the various Zionist groups.

Senator Fulbright: For what purpose?

Mr. Hamlin: These were payments that had been made for many, many years to the Zionist groups in this country as partial reimbursement to them for expenses they had, particularly in connection with their publications, and their house organs, to assist in the fundraising campaigns for Israel.

Senator Fulbright: Then it is quite clear, if I understand you, that the Jewish Agency Executive in this manner uses the American Zionist Council as a conduit for the dissemination of funds in this country?

Mr. Hamlin: The American Zionist Council accepted these funds and turned them over to Zionist groups. That is right.

Senator Fulbright: For various purposes.

Mr. Hamlin: For the purposes I stated. Specifically to reimburse them for expenses in connection with their publications and other services they rendered to assist the fundraising campaigns for Israel.

Senator Fulbright: Could you tell me why the Agency didn't pay this money directly to the various ultimate users of the funds? Why did it use the Zionist Council as a conduit?

Mr. Hamlin: The Zionist Council is itself composed of most of these same groups that received these payments. There was a closer connection and relationship between the Zionist Council and these groups than there was between the American Section and these groups. And, secondly, as I stated earlier, we hoped that the Council would take over these responsibilities eventually from us; that is, the Council from funds that it would receive from American sources would be able to take over this responsibility from us.

Senator Fulbright: Mr. Hamlin—

Mr. Hamlin: This was a hope.

Senator Fulbright: Let me make it clear. You have stated before that the Jewish Agency, Jerusalem supplied these funds, didn't it, to the Zionist Council?

Mr. Hamlin: The Jewish Agency-American Section provided these—the Jewish Agency, Jerusalem—pardon me, sir. The Jewish Agency—we receive all our funds, the American Section receives all its funds, from the Jewish Agency, Jerusalem.

Senator Fulbright: Well, in this case that I just went over, I hope—there are so many of these interlocking organizations, I would like to keep some of them straight. Didn't we just agree that the Jewish Agency, Jerusalem paid $62,000 to the American Zionist Council?

Mr. Hamlin: No. The Jewish Agency, Jerusalem, I believe—

Senator Fulbright: I mean, gave it to them as a conduit; didn't you just agree to that a moment ago?

Mr. Hamlin: Yes, sir, I did.

Senator Fulbright: Then please don't say no. You completely confuse the record. I am coming to the point that it wasn't for their personal use, but they used the Zionist Council as a conduit for this money, didn't they?

Mr. Hamlin: Yes, I stated that.

Senator Fulbright: Didn't this, in effect, avoid the clear requirement that would have applied if they paid it directly, that they would have to report it under the Foreign Agents Registration Act?

Mr. Hamlin: That the recipient's organizations would have to register under the Foreign Agents Registration Act? Do I understand you correctly?

Senator Fulbright: That the Agency would have to disclose this payment, wouldn't they?

Mr. Hamlin: The Agency did disclose those payments, sir, in our filings to the Department of Justice.

Senator Fulbright: To the Zionist Council?

Mr. Hamlin: These payments were included, yes, sir.

Senator Fulbright: But you have already said it wasn't for the Zionist Council's purposes. It was for somebody else's purpose, and this was concealed by this method of reporting, wasn't it?

Mr. Hamlin: In our filings with the Department of Justice we stated that these payments were being turned over to the Council to subvent, to assist, the Zionist groups in the public—to help them provide services to the campaign, to assist fundraising for Israel through their publications. That purpose was clearly stated.

Senator Fulbright: Now, Mr. Hamlin—

Mr. Hamlin: Excuse me, sir.

Senator Fulbright: Mr. Hamlin, let me correct you before you go too far: even that was only done last October after this committee started these studies. You had no itemization prior to that at all: did you?

Mr. Hamlin: Prior to that—

Senator Fulbright: None at all?

Mr. Hamlin: That is right, sir.

Senator Fulbright: And this was only started last fall, but even under that arrangement of itemization it doesn't show what this money was really used for—if it is used for propaganda, or an effort to influence the Congress, or so on. It does not appear in that itemization because of the use of a conduit; does it?

I only wanted to see how this operates, and I can assure you, because I raise my voice doesn't exhibit any anger; you asked me to.

I am not trying to argue with you; I just wanted to try to get the record clear.
Go ahead.

Mr. Boukstein: Mr. Chairman—

Senator Fulbright: All right, Mr. Boukstein.

Mr. Boukstein: Mr. Chairman, it is clear to me there was a misunderstanding; he thought you were talking of a recent period.

Now, I assume that you were addressing your question to the earlier period. At that time, it is absolutely correct that the reports to the Department of Justice were in summary form, a lump-sum payment, certain amount stated to affiliated organizations and the ultimate recipients of the funds were not stated in that report.

Senator Fulbright: What was done with the money was not clear at all from the report, was it? Isn't that correct?

Mr. Boukstein: If the Department of Justice wanted more information, they could have got it.

Senator Fulbright: Well, do you think the law puts upon the Department the full responsibility for your disclosure?

Mr. Boukstein: No, Mr. Chairman; I don't mean that at all. As I think I stated to you in the executive session, we followed the method of reporting which we thought was adequate.

Then, in 1962 when the Department felt that this—for some reason felt that this method should be changed, they asked us, and we changed, and the details are being reported since that time.

Senator Fulbright: I think, being as objective as I know how, that under the Foreign Agents Registration Act, the intervention of the Zionist Council between the actual user of the money—that is, the fellow or the organization that actually uses it for payment for work—seems to be to be merely a way of avoiding a disclosure here that should be disclosed as to what is done with the money, because the Zionist Council itself does not register and does not itemize what it does with the money.

Mr. Boukstein: Mr. Chairman—this is one, what you are saying is a possible inference; but, as I told you during the—and as the witness has stated time and again during the executive session, there never was any attempt to conceal. There was no reason for concealing. If you contend that the Act is not perfect, I as a lawyer may agree with you. You take, for instance, the labeling provision. I, as a registered lawyer for a foreign principal, can write a letter to the *New York Times*, and if I wrote on the subject matter which is connected with my work as a lawyer for the Jewish Agency, let's say, I would have to label that letter.

But the *New York Times* wouldn't have to, if it printed my letter, would not have to reprint the labeling of that letter.

Now it is a very moot question as to whether the recipient of funds originating from a foreign principal would have to be designated; now maybe that is one of the things that you would like to rectify.

Senator Fulbright: Exactly, Mr. Boukstein. This is one of the very interesting questions that has arisen not only in this connection but in some other connections as to the application of this Act.

In other words, is it going to be possible to avoid the real operation of the Act, and its disclosure, by the use of intermediaries where you give it to A, and A gives it to B, and B gives it to C, and C finally uses it, but by that time nothing whatever is disclosed as to what he does with it. This is exactly the point I am trying to develop as to how it operates, because your very able and acute legal mind has created some situations here that are very difficult for me to understand, and I have tried to.

There are so many different affiliated organizations with very similar names, and it is almost impossible for me to follow just what happens. This is one of the questions.

If this can be done successfully, it would seem to me that a very drastic revision of the law is called for.

Mr. Boukstein: Mr. Chairman, I would like to say that I think that the purpose of your inquiry is justified, because I do think that this law does require some bringing up to date in a number of respects, and I think this committee has done a very good job.

Senator Fulbright: Well, I am not sure we have. I am not sure I am a bit more enlightened that I was when I started. I am afraid I am more confused.

But this seems to me to be a case of the one who registers is largely a sort of conduit and really doesn't do very much. You have to go much further abroad to find out what actually finally is done with the money which comes from the Agency.[59]

    Senator Fulbright continued to grapple with the issue of the movement of money through "conduits," because the proper term for what was actually occurring had not yet entered mainstream English usage: *money laundering.* Money laundering, or the process of cleaning up dirty money to appear legitimate in law, is an apt description for the conduit network uncovered by Fulbright and his researchers. The practice of setting up or using existing entities to execute specific financial transactions concealing the source, identity, destination, and ultimate usage of money is common in the underworld and the informal economy. [60]

    In the past, the term "money laundering" was strictly applied only to organized-crime-related financial transactions. Its modern-day definition has been expanded by government regulators such as the United States Office of the Comptroller of the Currency. A broader definition is also endorsed by the Financial Action Task Force, a Paris-based multinational group formed in 1989 by the Group of Seven industrialized nations to foster international action against money laundering. Working definitions now encompass any financial transaction that generates a value or an asset as the result of an illegal act. While this can involve actions such as tax evasion or false accounting, it can also encompass the misuse or misdirection of tax-exempt funds. The act of erecting conduit and intermediary corporations to avoid due disclosure to regulatory entities (in this case, the Foreign Agents Registration office of the Department of Justice) fits within the modern definitions of money laundering.

    Money laundering is now recognized as a crime practiced not just by gangsters, but also individuals, small and large corporations, corrupt officials, charities, and even corrupt states. Money laundering was rampant in America's Prohibition era, though tax evasion charges were what eventually brought down money-laundering master Al Capone. Mobster Meyer Lansky began transferring funds from Florida casinos overseas, eventually acquiring an empire of shell and holding companies anchored to a Swiss bank he purchased to take advantage of 1934 Swiss Banking Act secrecy.

    The first popular references to money laundering surfaced a decade after Fulbright gaveled the hearings to a close—specifically during the Watergate scandal. It was revealed that US President Richard Nixon's "Committee to Re-elect the President" moved illegal campaign contributions to Mexico, then brought the money back through a Miami-based corporation. Britain's *Guardian* newspaper dryly referred to that process as "laundering." The transcript reveals Fulbright's "hunch" that something very wrong was going on between US charitable entities and the Jewish Agency. Four decades later, former Israeli prosecutor Talia Sason would fully reveal the operational criminal details first explored by Fulbright—far too late to do anything about it.

Vulnerabilities of the Early Israel Lobby

The American Zionist Committee was often cash-strapped and on the verge of insolvency. While AIPAC would later flaunt its financial muscle and repeatedly state that it only used non-tax-deductible funds raised from American donors to finance legislative initiatives on Capitol Hill, the early years of the Israel lobby were markedly different.

On April 15, 1960, Gottlieb Hammer, the executive vice chairman of the Jewish Agency, received an urgent appeal from Rabbi Jerome Unger, executive director of the American Zionist Council. Even after receiving $84,500 from the Jewish Agency, Unger was desperate for funds to cover, among other things, the American Zionist Council payroll.

Urgent Appeals for Jewish Agency Funds
(Source: Fulbright Hearings[61])

> ...In addition to the sum of $5,581.73 noted above as still due to the American Zionist Council on the balance for the fiscal year ending March 31, 1960, I must call to your attention that during the month of April, thus far, we have received absolutely nothing on the account of the new fiscal year. As a result, our accounts are in deficit. In other words, we are unable to pay bills and shall be unable to meet payroll expenses.
>
> Pending new arrangements for the fiscal year beginning April 1, 1960, may I urge that every effort be made to remit to us enough monies at least to cover payroll and minimum estimating expenses.
>
> With kindest regards, I am Sincerely yours,
>
> Rabbi Jerome Unger, Executive Director

Overseas cash was urgently needed to keep Israel's US influence campaign moving. US fundraisers had to perpetually flog potential givers to the cause because "few contributors spontaneously send their checks in each year."[62] Potential collaborators who were wary of Zionism could become interested in Israel and then become allies of the cause, but only if enough financial resources were available. The American Zionist Council's Department of Information field report stressed the importance of ongoing funding for public relations programs to get Americans interested in Israel on board:

> "The intensification of our public relations work within the local communities and the strengthening of the movement at grassroots level, and (2) the establishment of committees of volunteers on the national level. We now have six such committees made up of men and

women who are highly skilled and trained professionals in their respective fields and who volunteer their services because of a deep interest in Israel and concern for its welfare. *Although few are committed Zionists in the traditional sense of the word, they are happy to function under the aegis of a Zionist body such as ours....*"[63]

Not all conduit operations proceeded smoothly. The startup operations funded by Jewish Agency seed money were threatened by potential backlash from blind conduit operations such as the Rabinowitz Foundation, which was unwittingly laundering funds for an early Israel lobby public policy "think tank." In a letter to Senator Fulbright, the administrator of the Rabinowitz Foundation explained how his foundation became a conduit supplying $20,000 per year in Israeli government funds to Dr. Benjamin Shwadran, director of a startup Israel lobby public policy "think tank" called the Council on Middle East Affairs and its publication, *Middle Eastern Affairs.*[64]

Rabinowitz Foundation Letter to Senator Fulbright

(Source: Fulbright Hearings[65]*)*

Louis M. Rabinowitz Foundation, Inc.
New York, N.Y., July 29, 1963

Senator J.W. Fulbright
Chairman, Committee on Foreign Relations

Dear Senator Fulbright: You were kind enough to send me excerpts of testimony presented in executive session on May 23 before the Committee on Foreign Relations of the U.S. Senate in which the name of the Louis M. Rabinowitz Foundation was mentioned. I am glad to have this opportunity to comment on the testimony.

The Louis M. Rabinowitz Foundation was created many years ago by my father. Its assets consist of a number of patents and its income is derived almost exclusively from royalties on those patents. It is not a very large foundation, at least in comparison to the Ford Foundation and similar institutions. Its total income has been in the neighborhood of $150,000 a year and under the applicable Treasury regulations an equivalent amount has been disbursed in grants each year.

The powers of the foundation are, generally speaking, to make grants for religious, educational, or charitable purposes. In accordance with this policy, the foundation has, over a period of many years, made grants to large numbers of educational institutions, it has made substantial grants to a number of charities, and it has given grants for research work in history, archaeology, political science, economics and related fields.

I succeeded to the presidency of the foundation on the death of my father in 1957. Shortly thereafter, a new board of trustees was elected. I had had no connection with the administration of foundation affairs prior to that date. In examining the foundation records I found that the foundation had been receiving funds from the American Zionist Council and had been making equivalent grants to the Council on Middle Eastern Affairs.[66] Mr. Schwadran explained to me that this was an accommodation by my father arising out of his deep interest in Middle Eastern affairs and that the practice had been followed for a number of years.

Out of consideration for my father's interest in the matter, the board decided to continue the practice, particularly since there was no resultant depletion in the funds of the foundation and contributions to the work of the Council on Middle Eastern Affairs appeared to fall within the framework and the purposes and powers of the foundation. We had no knowledge that the Jewish Agency had any role in the situation whatsoever and it was certainly never suggested to us that the Jewish Agency was the ultimate source of funds going to the Council on Middle Eastern Affairs.

In or about February 1963 my secretary advised me that she had received a telephone call to the effect that in the future the foundation would receive some funds directly from the Jewish Agency instead of from the American Zionist Council. Frankly, I paid very little attention to the change; it had no significance to me and I did not even advise the board. I did not know at the time that the Jewish Agency was a representative of the Israeli Government.

Shortly after the hearing before your committee, Mr. Boukstein called me and advised me that the question had been raised before the committee as to the role of the foundation in the financing of the Council on Middle Eastern Affairs. He also mentioned the fact that the Jewish Agency was a representative of the Israeli Government. He said he was calling the matter to my attention because he thought I ought to know about it: he expressed no opinion at all as to the course of conduct the foundation ought to follow in the future. I, therefore, consulted with the board of the foundation and with counsel and we agreed that the foundation did not wish to be a conduit of funds from the Israeli Government or the Jewish Agency and I so advised Mr. Schwadran. He assured me that neither the Israeli Government or the American Zionist Council had ever influenced the policies of his publication, and I believe that to be true. I have read the publication occasionally and it seems to be rather academic in nature and quite objective in its editorial policy. We, nevertheless, felt that, under the circumstances, the foundation no longer cared to receive funds from any source for transmittal to the Council on Middle Eastern Affairs. We advised Mr. Schwadran to that effect about 3 weeks ago.

Yours sincerely,

Victor Rabinowitz

Fulbright began interrogating Jewish Agency legal counsel Boukstein about the blind conduit operation funding the think tank.

Senator Fulbright: This illustrates to me how not even the conduit, much less the Department of Justice or Congress, know the origins of the money and what it is used for in circumstances of this kind.

I think it does present a very important question to the committee as to how this might be dealt with in future legislation. That is why I was trying to develop the point.

Mr. Boukstein. Mr. Chairman, inasmuch as my name is mentioned in this letter would you permit me to make a few observations on it?

Senator Fulbright: Certainly.

Mr. Boukstein: In the first place, I would like to state very clearly and most emphatically that—

Senator Lausche: Which paragraph are you directing our attention to?

Mr. Boukstein: I will point that out in a minute, Senator. While it is true that I invited Mr. Rabinowitz to tell him that the name of the foundation was brought up in the executive session—I felt it was only right and proper I should do so—it is absolutely incorrect that I told him that the Jewish Agency, as he says in the third paragraph of his letter on page 2, it is absolutely incorrect that I said that the Jewish Agency was a representative of the Israeli Government.

I couldn't have said it. No one knows better than I that it isn't so. It just isn't a fact. He just got mixed up on that.

Senator Fulbright: That is a matter of opinion, isn't it really? It is not a factual matter.

Mr. Boukstein: No, Mr. Chairman, I am sorry, this is not a matter of opinion.

Senator Fulbright: Here again I think the distinction between the strictly legal relationships with the corporate structure is what you are talking about, isn't it?

Mr. Boukstein: No, I am talking about a fact.

Senator Fulbright: What is a fact in this connection? To a corporate lawyer, what to a lawyer is a fact may not be to a layman, isn't that correct?

Mr. Boukstein: Well, Mr. Chairman, I think there are some facts which are facts to lawyers and to laymen as well.

Senator Fulbright: I am only inviting you to elaborate this connection if you will.

Mr. Boukstein: I would be glad to. The Jewish Agency is an independent body consisting of representatives of Zionist organizations from all over the world, all over the free world, let me say. They have their own constitutional authorities. There is a Congress which meets on the average of approximately every four years. It elects its own committees. It consists of designated or elected delegates from all over the world.

The Congress does not have any delegates from the Government of Israel. The majority of the people at the Congress, the majority of delegates are not residents of Israel. The Executive of the Jewish Agency for Israel in Jerusalem is elected by the Congress. It is responsible to the Congress and to its, the

Zionist Congress, and to its institutions. It has a formal legal agreement with the Government of Israel delineating its operations in Israel which it would have to have in any country where it would operate.

Obviously, taking into account the type of activity that the Jewish Agency is engaged in, immigration, and absorption, resettlement, housing, and so forth, it must have, perforce, it must have if it is to succeed, the closest liaison with the Government, with the host government. But it is not controlled by, it is not dominated by, it is to some extent aided as it should be, by the Government, but it is completely independent, and therefore, Mr. Chairman, it isn't a matter of opinion at all. It is a matter of fact.

Senator Fulbright: Then, may I ask you, is Rabinowitz—he said you told him it was, will you deny that you told him it was?

Mr. Boukstein: I do, Mr. Chairman.

Senator Fulbright: Well, that is the main fact of the question.

Mr. Boukstein: I would like to make one—

Senator Fulbright: Mr. Rabinowitz is not being truthful, in your opinion?

Mr. Boukstein: I didn't say he was not being truthful. I said he misunderstood what I said.

Senator Fulbright: He wrote this committee within 2 days that you told him.

Mr. Boukstein: I am sure if Mr. Rabinowitz were here he would make the correction and if it pleases the Chair, I will see to it that he does make the correction. I never told him, because I couldn't have told him, it isn't a fact, that the Agency is a representative of the Israel Government. It just isn't so. I would like to make, if I may, one other observation about his letter.

Now, it is not correct that the Rabinowitz Foundation did not at any time know that the source of funds originated with the Jewish Agency. Mr. Rabinowitz, the young Mr. Rabinowitz, who is the present head of the foundation, may not have known. But his father surely did know, no question about it, and he died not so very long ago.

Now, one other thing, it is our information, and I will be glad to check it for you, Mr. Chairman, that in addition to funds which we made available, which the Jewish Agency-American Section made available for the Rabinowitz Foundation, the Rabinowitz foundation from its own funds made some contributions to the Council for Middle Eastern Affairs.

Senator Fulbright: You say recently died. According to this letter or maybe this is inaccurate, do you know when his father died? Mr. Rabinowitz thought he died in 1957.

Mr. Boukstein: That is not too long ago.

Senator Fulbright: That is six years ago. I would think he would have time to become acquainted with what the foundation is doing.

Mr. Boukstein: Well, apparently he didn't.

Senator Fulbright: Then he doesn't pay attention to his affairs.

Mr. Boukstein: It could be.

Senator Fulbright: It could be. Well, I don't wish to belabor the matter, but at least this man, and I am not personally acquainted with Mr. Rabinowitz, but as soon as he discovered the origin of the funds, took the view that he did not wish to be a conduit of such funds and I think this could happen on other foundations, if they do not know where the origin of the funds is, could it not? Mr. Boukstein: It could.[67]

Fulbright appeared to believe that the "shell corporation" arrangement created by Boukstein was principally an artifice created to hide activity and move money to undisclosed purposes. To the layman, it would simply appear that in spite of the corporate entities, Israel was setting up and funding its lobbying shop in the US. But Fulbright did not choose to linger on the blind conduit backlash issue: the inquiry moved on to the related question of Israel's support for US public policy think tanks that was raised in the Rabinowitz case.

Time would prove that Victor Rabinowitz was acutely observant in stating that the Council on Middle East Affairs was "academic in nature and quite objective in its editorial policy."[68] In fact, it was too objective and academic to be useful to AIPAC and the interests of the Israel lobby, which went through several permutations looking for the perfect public policy think tank solution. Although think tank pioneer the Brookings Institution had been around for 47 years at the time of the hearing, the Israel lobby was only beginning its foray into funding think tanks. This foray, which began with support for the Council on Middle East Affairs, would ultimately lead to the establishment of other Israel lobby think tanks as well as a "friendly takeover" of Brookings Institution Middle East policy research in 2002 by former AIPAC deputy research director Martin Indyk.

The "Retail Job": US Think Tanks

The Jewish Agency was interested in the public relations potential of favorable "scholarly research" and funded policy research by channeling funds through the American Zionist Council. The Council on Middle East Affairs was an early precursor to the plethora of Israel-centric modern-day "think tanks" that dominate policy debate and media coverage about the Middle East from Washington, DC. The Jewish Agency intended that seed money for favorable research publications with academic patina would result in a self-sustaining interdependency between lobbying organizations such as the American Zionist Committee and foundations with "credible, research-oriented" think tanks. Although the Council on Middle East Affairs did not grow to be as influential, powerful, and self-sustaining as expected, the Israel lobby and AIPAC would later leverage the lessons learned in forming, running, and even taking over influential think tanks.

Senator Fulbright: Again, I ask you what was the reason for making these payments through the American Zionist Council rather than directly to the Council on Middle East Affairs.

Gottlieb Hammer: We did it directly through the American Zionist Council, or if there had been no Zionist Council we would have urged domestic groups here to form one only because they were better equipped to carry on this broad program of information and education and this broad program of attempting to rally support for the cause of Israel and for the cause of refugee immigration much better than we could.

They were equipped to do it. They had representatives all over the United States. The American Zionist Council is made of up domestic—

Senator Fulbright: I understand that, but the Council on Middle East Affairs was in being, and it was doing the job. Why didn't you subsidize them directly rather than indirectly through the American Zionist Council? I don't understand why this was not a direct payment from you rather than—this entailed, it seemed to be, more unusual bookkeeping than necessary. I don't quite understand the motive for this procedure.

Gottlieb Hammer: Well Senator, it was one way of attempting to give the American Zionist Council increased stature, increased prestige, as the organization which is doing the overall job, and we had a general rule of not getting involved to the extent possible, in detailed operations. We tried to make a distinction between a wholesale job and a retail job.[69]

Disassociating think tanks and policy advocacy from the interests of the Israeli government in the perception of the American public would remain a challenge for the Jewish Agency and AIPAC over the next thirty years. AIPAC's Deputy Director of Research Martin Indyk would attempt to resolve the problem repeatedly. First he established the Washington Institute for Near East Affairs in 1984 with the help of major AIPAC fundraisers. Unsatisfied, Indyk would again try to escape the appearance of being tied to the Israel lobby by "carving out" a new Middle East Policy division at the near-century-old Brookings Institution with the help of $13 million in funding from Israeli-American media mogul Haim Saban,.

The old Council on Middle East Affairs became less relevant as years passed, though a similar-sounding entity was recently resuscitated for a key lobbying initiative that required a third-party front. Throughout its life, the think tank was referred to even by funders such as the Rabinowitz Foundation as the Council on Middle East**ern** Affairs, probably due to the name of its signature publication. Public relations firm Benador Associates, famous for handling a stable of neoconservative television pundits such as Richard Perle, Max Boot, Richard Pipes, Frank Gaffney, R. James Woolsey, Barry Rubin, and Lauri Mylroie, among others, obtained a high-profile briefing for the "Council on Middle **Eastern** Affairs" in September of 2002. The Council's "expert" was Dr. Khidir Hamza, an Iraqi dissident who claimed he once ran Saddam Hussein's nuclear program. Dr. Hamza gave a single speech to the House Armed Services Committee, providing wildly deceptive and false "evidence" that Iraq's emergence as a nuclear power was imminent:

The nuclear weapons program is now almost complete waiting for the enrichment sector, which makes 90% of the program to finish its job and put together a working production facility. The bottlenecks in the enrichment are already resolved.[70]

The Council has since vanished as inexplicably as it reappeared.[71] During the course of the hearings, American Zionist Council propaganda efforts on behalf of the Israeli government weren't the only highlight. It was also discovered through Senate Foreign Relations Committee subpoenaed documents that the Jewish Agency acquired and owned the Jewish Telegraphic Agency (JTA) news service through a holding company. Fulbright explored the implications of this quasi-foreign-government media ownership in the US and the independence of the JTA in the August 2, 1963 hearing.

Control of the Jewish Telegraphic Agency

Many Americans believe that AIPAC exercises massive and unwarranted behind-the-scenes influence on top-tier American news media, particularly regarding content about the Middle East. As revealed in the contents of a never-before-published memo from Thomas W. Lippman, the Washington Post's former Middle East Bureau chief (discussed in chapter 5), that belief is empirically, though not universally, accurate.

In the early days, the Israel lobby had an even more direct influence on one particular media outlet—through direct ownership. During the hearings in both May and August, it was revealed in subpoenaed documents that the Jewish Agency owned a news company, the Jewish Telegraphic Agency. Many Jewish Telegraphic Agency wire service subscribers, typically community newspapers across the United States and their readers, were not aware of the takeover. Fulbright revealed that the Jewish Agency hid payments and filed deceptive FARA reports with Jewish Telegraph Agency cash flow reduced to a single non-descriptive line item of "Grants and Subventions."

Senator Fulbright: What proportion, if any, of the outstanding shares of the Jewish Telegraphic Agency did the Jewish Agency-American Section own?
Mr. Hamlin: The Jewish Agency-American Section owns all the shares of the JTA.
Senator Fulbright: What proportion of the outstanding shares of the Jewish Telegraphic News Agency, Inc. did the Jewish Agency-American Section own?
Mr. Hamlin: The Jewish Agency owns, if I may correct myself, the Jewish Agency owns all the shares of the JTNA, which, in turn, owns the JTA.

Senator Fulbright: Did the Jewish Agency-American Section render financial assistance to the Telegraphic Agency after April 1, 1960, as contemplated by your letter?

Mr. Hamlin: It did, sir.

Senator Fulbright: Can you supply the committee with a detailed accounting of all payments made by your Agency to the Telegraphic Agency from April 1, 1960 to the present day?

Mr. Hamlin: I can, sir.

Senator Fulbright: Did you report all these payments on your registration statement filed with the Department of Justice?

Mr. Hamlin: Yes, sir; we did.

Senator Fulbright: Did you report them as payments to the JTA?

Mr. Hamlin: Here we must refer to these documents again to be most accurate.

Mr. Boukstein: What particular period are you referring to, sir?

Senator Fulbright: April 1, 1960, to the present. They are in 6-month periods.

Mr. Hamlin: Sir, even without referring here to these documents for the details, I can tell you that for—up until about March of 1961, the details in our statements to the Justice Department did not indicate the recipients, the names of the recipients. They were bunched together under "Grants and Subventions."

Subsequent to that date, we submitted to the Justice Department detailed information naming all those organizations which received funds from us. Included from that date on was, of course, the Jewish Telegraphic Agency, all the grants made to the Jewish Telegraphic Agency.

Senator Fulbright: Itemized under that name?

Mr. Hamlin: Yes, sir.[72]

Fulbright explored the implications of this quasi-foreign-government ownership and the editorial independence of the Jewish Telegraphic Agency during the May 23 hearing.

Senator Fulbright: ...But you did, through the Telegraphic News Agency, of course, control the Jewish Telegraphic Agency? You had all the stock in the Jewish News Agency?

Hammer: Yes, sir, we had the voting shares, we owned the Agency that is right.

Senator Fulbright: And it in turn owned the voting shares of the Jewish Telegraphic Agency?

Hammer: Yes, sir. In this sense I should like, if I may, to comment on the term "controlled," and what it means.

We owned the shares. We never did exercise control in the sense of regular board meetings where there were votes. I know I was elected to the board, and I never attended, there never was a meeting in a long period of time. There was never any attempt on our part to influence or control the editorial policy of the JTA. *In fact, I recall having called the editor of the JTA once or twice to complain about what I felt was unfair treatment of some of the news items coming from Israel.*[73]

Hammer, the executive vice chairman of the Jewish Agency, would later correct the record in a letter stating that in spite of his contradictory statement, the Jewish Agency did not interfere in the "editorial policy" of the JTA. Fulbright went on to ask Hammer whether the Jewish Agency's acquisition of a controlling interest in the JTA was ever properly disclosed in the United States.

Senator Fulbright: Was that acquisition of the stock of the Jewish Telegraphic News Agency reported to the Department of Justice under question 12 (b) of the supplemental registration statement relating to changes in registrants control over other organizations?
Mr. Hammer: I do not recall, sir.
Senator Fulbright: Was there any public notice made in any fashion that the Jewish Agency had acquired the ownership of the Jewish Telegraphic News Agency and the Jewish Telegraphic Agency?
Hammer: I do not recall any public notice, although the matter was generally known to the Council of Jewish Federations & Welfare Funds, which so informed its members, its constituent members, 234 communities throughout the country, and other national Jewish organizations which were aware of this situation.
Senator Fulbright: Did this Agency have any subscribers in this country?
Hammer: This agency has subscribers of individuals as well as Anglo-Jewish newspapers and the wire services.
Senator Fulbright: In this country?
Hammer: In this country.
Senator Fulbright: As well as abroad?
Hammer: As well as abroad, sir.
Senator Fulbright: Were those subscribers informed that the ownership of this agency rested with your agency?
Hammer: I would not know, sir. I did not interfere in the operations of the JTA.[74]

To this day, the Jewish Telegraphic Agency continues to actively cover events and syndicate news, particularly policy issues in Washington, DC. While AIPAC and other parts of the Israel lobby are powerful media players, they have no need of actually owning news media outlets. Access to top-tier corporate media through continuation of highly active public relations, presence on Madison Avenue, and sympathetic media executives, some who are actually board members, has dramatically increased message placement since the days of direct ownership.

Israeli Consulate Financing of the *Israel Digest*

In addition to financing Si Kenen's *Near East Report*, the Jewish Telegraphic Agency, and the activities of the American Zionist Council's "Department of Information," the Jewish Agency was also jointly financing, along with the Israeli Consulate, an Israel government propaganda newsletter, the *Israel Digest*. Even in the 1960s, the *Israel Digest* was actively pushing weapons of mass destruction "buttons" in ways many American readers today may find oddly reminiscent of the pre-Iraq-invasion WMD claims.

Senator Fulbright: Are you acquainted with a publication called the *Israel Digest*?

Mr. Hamlin. Yes, sir, I am.

Senator Fulbright: Who publishes it?

Mr. Hamlin: The Jewish Agency.

Senator Fulbright: Do you finance it?

Mr. Hamlin: Yes, sir, we do.

Senator Fulbright: Does the Israel Consulate finance it also?

Mr. Hamlin: No, sir: the Israel Consulate purchases a number of subscriptions of this publication and furnishes us with a list of persons that they want to have this publication sent to. And they reimburse us for those subscriptions.

Senator Fulbright: Do you know what percentage of your total?

Mr. Hamlin: The percentage is about 50 percent. I would say, of the total circulation, or perhaps more.

Senator Fulbright: How do you distinguish when I ask you if they finance it, and you say no, they just purchase this product, what in your mind makes that distinction?

Mr. Hamlin: How I make that distinction?

Senator Fulbright: Yes, what is the difference in fact between directly contributing and in buying their subscriptions and sending them wherever you like? It would seem to me it is all the same thing.

Mr. Boukstein: I am not sure I understand your question.

Senator Fulbright: Well, it doesn't matter. I show you copies of three pages from the cash receipts journal of your Agency, supplied under subpoena, and ask you if you have seen these pages before? How much of your subscriptions for this Digest do they amount to?"

Mr. Hamlin: Are you asking how much we received from the Consulate, sir?

Senator Fulbright: How much is each one worth, I mean, what is the price?

Mr. Hamlin: I believe that at that time it was $1.50 or $2 per subscription.

Senator Fulbright: You will notice on these pages dated December, 1961, carries a time of "12/15—Consulate General of Israel, Israel Digest, $5000." What does that mean?

Mr. Hamlin: Oh, yes, this is the payment to us.

Senator Fulbright: Payment to you by the Consulate General?

Mr. Hamlin: That is right, for these subscriptions.

Senator Fulbright: For subscriptions?

Mr. Hamlin: For the subscriptions they purchased from us of the *Israel Digest*, which we mailed to a list of individuals they gave us.

Senator Fulbright: Is that 5,000 subscriptions?

Mr. Hamlin No, that was more than 5,000 subscriptions, I believe, because this was part of the payment for that year. This was not the total payment for that year.

Senator Fulbright: How much do you receive each year?

Mr. Hamlin: Pardon me?

Senator Fulbright: How much do you receive each year?

Mr. Hamlin: We have received from the Israel Consulate around $10,000 to $15,000 a year for these subscriptions.

Senator Fulbright: Can you tell us how much you received from the Israel Consulate in a normal year, say, last year, for all purposes, from every source. Is it large?

Mr. Hamlin: Sir, from the Israel Consulate we received money for the *Digest*, the $10,000 to $15,000 I mentioned, and it provides for the Jewish minority research project, and these two projects and the later sum of $5,000. These are the only two sums we received from the Israel Government offices.

Senator Fulbright: Did the Israel Consulate send you a mailing list that you mailed out these *Digests*?

Mr. Hamlin: We do the mailing, if that is your question.

Senator Fulbright: They send you a list.

Mr. Hamlin: That is right. We do the mailing from our office. We arrange to have it printed and we have a mailing list in our office.

Senator Fulbright: I see. Well, the second item here was March 1962, was just a little over a year ago, "Consulate, *Israel Digest*, $9000." Then in June of 1962, the *Israel Digest*, $1,210.86. Who paid for the mailing of this, Mr. Hamlin? Do you pay for the mailing?

Mr. Hamlin: Sir?

Senator Fulbright: Do you pay for the mailing?

Mr. Hamlin: Certainly, we mail this thing out physically.

Senator Fulbright: I see.

Mr. Hamlin: We pay for the mailing. The Consulate reimburses us, sir, for all costs in connection with mailing of that number of subscriptions from the list they give us. And we bear all the costs of that and they reimburse us for that.

Senator Fulbright: I don't suppose you could be called the agent in mailing this out for them, could, you?

Mr. Hamlin: An agent? I think they were buying services from us.

Senator Fulbright: I see.

Mr. Boukstein: Mr. Chairman, I think it should be stated for the record that this publication is labeled in accordance with the requirements of the Foreign Agents Registration Act of 1938.

Senator Fulbright: Well, I notice that it says, the label is as follows: "A copy of this material is filed with the Department of Justice where the required registration statement of the Jewish Agency-American Section, Inc., as an agent of the Jewish Agency for Israel, Jerusalem, Israel, under the Foreign Agents Registration Act of 1938, as amended, is available for public inspection. Registration does not indicate approval of this material by the U.S. Government." Do you think this label accurately describes the relationship between the Jewish Agency and the *Israel Digest* to those who read the Digest?

Mr. Hamlin: Yes, sir.

Senator Fulbright: Do you think any who read that know that the Government of Israel paid for it?

Mr. Hamlin: They would have no way of knowing.

Senator Fulbright: Don't you think they ought to know?[75]

Cartoon from the Israel Digest, Page 1 Vol. 4

(Source: Fulbright Hearing Transcript[76])

NUCLEAR WARHEAD

Inside Nasser's Egypt weapons of mass destruction— including types banned by international law are being developed with the aid of German scientists and technicians in order to launch a war of extermination against Israel

The *Israel Digest*'s assertion that Egypt was developing "weapons of mass destruction" was an early step in what would become a central and ongoing campaign by Israel lobby think tanks and pundits to assert that Israel and the US were under continual threat of nuclear, chemical, and biological attack from Israel's enemies.

The 1960 Jewish Agency/US Reorganization

The vast reorganization in the 1960s that took Si Kenen directly off the Jewish Agency payroll while maintaining funding for essentially the same lobbying activity was a result of two developments. The first was that Jewish Agency "pump priming" for fundraising campaigns, propaganda, and political initiatives in the United States would become less important as American groups took up the reins and began self-sustaining fundraising operations. Organizations that engaged in propaganda, fundraising, and lobbying on behalf of Israel did not want any appearance of "foreign control" that would necessitate foreign agent registration beyond the minimal registrations and deceptive filings they had already made. By appearing to be autonomous, though deeply interlinked, American operations such as the American Zionist Council and AIPAC could build the Council on Near East Affairs, *Near East Report* and other nonprofit corporations under the rubric of "Americans lobbying on behalf of their own domestic interests." This earlier reorganization meant that by the time the Fulbright hearing was convened, the ground had already shifted beneath it. The Senate Foreign Relations Committee was armed with subpoenaed documents such as canceled payment vouchers from the Jewish Agency indirectly to Si Kenen, embarrassing and detailed conduit account information, and questions about subscription payments made directly from the Israeli Consulate and the Jewish Agency. But AIPAC and Kenen were already moving on to their next organizational structure and developmental phase for launching new initiatives in the United States. This would include influencing key elections through AstroTurf PACs to preclude the likelihood of another Fulbright-like inquiry curtailing or even investigating AIPAC's behind-the-scenes operations.

Fulbright Internationalism and the Neocons

The transcripts of Fulbright's investigation into the Israel lobby may someday be considered among his greatest achievements in public disclosure as well as one of America's greatest policy related law enforcement failures. His simple, pointed questions pierced the elaborate corporate and public relations veil of obfuscation that had been constructed entirely to hide the obvious. Was the Jewish Agency really much like the Red Cross (as claimed by its executive),[77] or more like a branch of the Israeli government? Was the financial support provided by the Jewish Agency and Israeli Consulate to the American Zionist Council and Si Kenen for newsletter publication and distribution a disinterested, arm's-length "service purchase" for "subscriptions," or was it covert support for lobbying and Israeli government propaganda? Did the United Jewish Appeal and American Zionist Council function like normal American charitable organizations or opaque money-launderers? Did the 1960 Israel lobby reorganization prompted by friendly warnings from Treasury Undersecretary Fred Scribner in 1959[78] fundamentally and suddenly reverse the power and reporting relationship of US Israel lobby members and entities in Israel, while erasing former close relationships among US organizations and former employees? Discerning readers of the entire set of Fulbright transcripts should have little trouble making up their own minds about these questions if they take an honest approach to the relevant documents.

Fulbright retired from the Senate in 1974 after finally being defeated by Governor Dale Bumpers in the Democratic primary. During that election year, the Anti-Defamation League, an American offshoot of B'nai B'rith linked to the Jewish Agency through the World Zionist Organization, attacked Senator Fulbright, labeling him "consistently unkind to Israel and our supporters in this country." Bumpers received significant campaign financial support from the Israel lobby, which did not yet have the national influence and infrastructure to swing the outcomes of many key elections nationwide.

Fulbright died in Washington, DC of a heart attack at the age of 89 in 1995. This year was an important milestone in the rise of the hard-line Israel-centric neoconservative power bloc in Washington. The bloc included the Project for a New American Century, a group of ideologues and operatives fundamentally opposed to the power and role of international organizations, multilateralism, and the respect for international law nurtured by Fulbright. In his seminal 1967 book *The Arrogance of Power*, Fulbright eloquently emphasized his core difference with the emerging neoconservative doctrine bent on redefining conservatism and establishing a radical new role for the US in the world, including the military reforming of the Middle East to the benefit of Israel and allegedly the US:

> Power tends to confuse itself with virtue and a great nation is particularly susceptible to the idea that its power is a sign of God's favor, conferring upon it a special responsibility for other nations—to make them richer and happier and wiser, to remake them, that is, in its own shining image. Power confuses itself with virtue and tends also to take itself for omnipotence. Once imbued with the idea of a mission, a great nation easily assumes that it has the means as well as the duty to do God's work.[79]

Law is the essential foundation of stability and order both within societies and in international relations. As a conservative power, the United States has a vital interest in upholding and expanding the reign of law in international relations. Insofar as international law is observed, it provides us with stability and order and with a means of predicting the behavior of those with whom we have reciprocal legal obligations. When we violate the law ourselves, whatever short-term advantage may be gained, we are obviously encouraging others to violate the law; we thus encourage disorder and instability and thereby do incalculable damage to our own long-term interests.[80]

Fulbright was among the most vocal investigators of the Israel lobby, but he was not alone in his concerns. As early as 1970, some critics such as Rabbi Elmer Berger were also beginning to question how long it would be before resentments voiced by Fulbright about the subordination of US interests to a foreign power created a broad backlash.

The real political-economic question is how long all parties concerned—the Fulbrights, the US Government generally, the American people—will take kindly to a subsidy for a policy of Israeli occupation [of Arab lands] with which the United Status in its own interests, and the interests of peace, is in opposition"[81]

Those active in building a US-based Israel lobby had little to fear. No effective political opposition or law enforcement had yet appeared on the horizon.

Two: Economic Espionage

Since the 1960s AIPAC has built significant intelligence-gathering operations in Congress and within many US government agencies. Although AIPAC would disagree with even asking the question, one decade old survey of the Congress alleged that "80 percent of the members of Congress now have former AIPAC interns on their staffs."[82] Congressional staffers are willing to go beyond intelligence gathering to formulate and modify policy in ways that benefit Israel. This does not always take place at the level of elected officials. Morris Amitay, a former head of AIPAC, once candidly outlined the importance of "staff-level" contacts to move initiatives across Congress:

> There are a lot of guys at the working level up here [on Capitol Hill]...who happen to be Jewish, who are willing...to look at certain issues in terms of their Jewishness....These are all guys who are in a position to make the decision in these areas for those senators....You can get an awful lot done just at the staff level.[83]

Congress no longer resists many Israel lobby initiatives guided by AIPAC, no matter how damaging they are to US interests. Unfortunately for some US industries, ongoing Israeli industrial espionage, violations of US pharmaceutical patents,[84] and trafficking in purloined US military technology have led to major losses and problems for export-oriented industries.

> Israel has provided sensitive military technology to potential rivals like China, in what the State Department inspector-general called "a systematic and growing pattern of unauthorized transfers." According to the General Accounting Office, Israel also "conducts the most aggressive espionage operations against the US of any ally." In addition to the case of Jonathan Pollard, who gave Israel large quantities of classified material in the early 1980s (which it reportedly passed on to the Soviet Union in return for more exit visas for Soviet Jews), a new controversy erupted in 2004 when it was revealed that a key Pentagon official called Larry Franklin had passed classified information to an Israeli diplomat. Israel is hardly the only country that spies on the US, but its willingness to spy on its principal patron casts further doubt on its strategic value.[85]

This embedded foreign interest group had one particularly negative effect on bilateral trade as a result of actions AIPAC took against the United

States during the negotiation of its very first free trade agreement. In this case, Israel, already known to be heavily involved in industrial espionage against the United States, benefited from covert actions in order to become the beneficiary of what has proven to be a decidedly costly "free trade agreement." The FTA could not have been negotiated without Israel's lobby using the US's own confidential information against it. Unfortunately for the US, that is exactly what happened.

Negotiating the US-Israel Free Trade Agreement with Material Inside Information

AIPAC's most egregious act of documented economic espionage against the United States was negotiating the very first US free trade deal using a strategy document purloined from the International Trade Commission. Like other cases, it was an act for which AIPAC paid no penalty, beyond admitting that it possessed the stolen ITC document. A decade and a half earlier, both Israel and its supporters in the US knew the advantage a highly preferential free trade agreement could bring to the Israeli economy, which was suffering chronic trade deficit and market access problems.

> Despite a booming economy, Israel's annual trade deficit has surged to nearly $1 billion, according to State Department figures, up 54 percent from a year ago. Military costs will consume 41 percent of the government's budget, straining even more the country's dwindling reserves of hard currency.[86]

While economists usually consider trade based on comparative advantage to be a "win-win" situation, this was not the driver of the US-Israel FTA. Going into the agreement, Israel had a lot to gain from an FTA with the US, but it was the weaker party, and under good-faith negotiations, would have been expected to yield greater benefits to the US.

The fact that Israel was first in line for an FTA before more powerful and important industrial nations offers further evidence that US interests were not the primary impetus of the FTA. If the broader economic interests of the American people and industry had been taken into consideration, Israel would not have even appeared on a list of the top ten nations with which the US should strike a trade deal. However, Israel's lobby, led by AIPAC, sought a "zero-sum game" of propping up a moribund economy that was overly burdened by military costs, collectivized kibbutzim, and state-operated industries. US industry was an easy target for AIPAC in Congress.

In order to drive the hardest bargain possible, AIPAC purloined detailed documents to negotiate against the US on behalf of Israel. Alerted to the crime, the FBI soon opened an investigation into how AIPAC came to possess confidential International Trade Commission documents.

The FBI is investigating how the major pro-Israel lobbying group obtained a copy of a classified document that spells out American negotiating strategy in trade talks with Israel, government officials said yesterday.

The document, a report from the International Trade Commission to U.S. Trade Representative William E. Brock, contains proprietary data supplied by American industries and other sensitive information for the negotiations, which began early this year.

Trade officials said the report would give Israel a significant advantage in the trade talks because it discloses how far the United States is willing to compromise on contested issues. Some of the proprietary information, moreover, could help Israeli businesses competing with U.S. companies, officials said.[87]

AIPAC was quick to trot out a "non-excuse excuse," but refused to divulge how it obtained the classified information, how it was used, or to whom it was passed.

A spokesman for the American Israel Public Affairs Committee (AIPAC), the principal pro-Israel lobbying group in this country, acknowledged that the organization had a copy of the report but said the lobbying group did nothing illegal.[88]

One U.S. trade official, who spoke only on condition he not be identified, said the document assessed "what U.S. products would be affected and how by a free trade agreement with Israel." As such, the document contained proprietary information supplied by American businesses on the understanding that it would not be publicly released, this official said.[89]

Only the passage of time has revealed how damaging this economic espionage has been to the US. The US footwear manufacturing industry was rendered powerless by the absolute advantage AIPAC and Israel obtained through the classified information and the lobby's lock on Congress. Breaking with industry norms and normal protocols of US corporate spokespeople, Fawn Evenson criticized the unfairness of the tainted process and AIPAC's central role:

"I think they've been very heavy-handed," FIA executive vice-president Fawn Evenson said, referring to AIPAC lobbying efforts, which last week successfully persuaded a substantial majority of the House Ways and Means Committee to reject amendments giving the U.S. footwear, leather goods, textile and apparel industries special protections against Israeli imports in the event a U.S.-Israeli free-trade zone is established for all other products.

"The lobbying (by AIPAC) on this bill has been so incredible you wouldn't believe it. They're making it very difficult for any member to do anything other than what they want him or her to do. I think they're going to lose some friends over this," Evenson said.[90]

AIPAC gave a public response that it would later repeat when caught with purloined secret information. The organization maintained that as long as it did not seek out data, having it and leveraging it against the United States government on behalf of Israel was not unlawful. AIPAC expressed no public remorse over the incident, and no staff members are known to have been fired over it.

At the lobbying committee, spokeswoman Lisa Behren said, "We had a copy and we turned it over to the U.S. government at their request."

She said she did not know how long the committee had the document, what use was made of it or who supplied it, but was aware that "we did not solicit it."[91]

Twenty years later, top AIPAC operatives would be indicted after FBI surveillance caught them soliciting highly classified national defense information from a Department of Defense source, selectively distributing it to compliant American news reporters, and ultimately passing it on to the state of Israel. The damage assessment for this most recent policy espionage involving Franklin, Rosen, and Weissman is not yet available. The passage of time has yielded a basis for the quantitative assessment of the US-Israel trade deal. The formerly balanced US-Israel trade has shifted into chronic deficit for the US.

1989-2006 US Trade Deficit with Israel
(Source: International Trade Administration, US Department of Commerce)

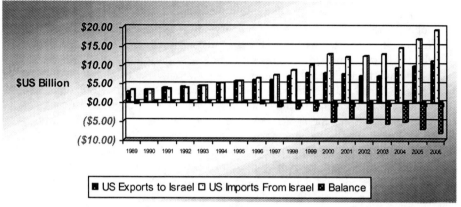

Rather than apologize or respond to questions raised by its possession of classified information, AIPAC fell back on a public relations strategy that would serve it well in the future. AIPAC maintained the position that US and Israeli interests were "the same," and that this severely corrupted trade relationship would ultimately benefit the United States.

> AIPAC, a Washington-based lobbying group that supports Israeli Government positions, has argued that American companies should benefit more than Israeli companies from the increased exports that would result from a U.S.-Israel free-trade zone.[92]

The FBI was unsuccessful in its investigation into the original source of the stolen ITC documents. Congress ultimately passed the free trade agreement in spite of the controversy and unfavorable negotiations. America's first free trade agreement has not been as beneficial for US exporters as AIPAC predicted. American manufacturers and stakeholders dependent on fair trade, or at least the economics of comparative advantage, suffered increasing deficits as Israeli industry, some of it heavily subsidized by the government, capitalized on an unmerited subsidy from American workers and industry. **The cumulative US trade deficit with Israel from 1989 to 2006 reached $47.5 billion.[ii]**

Many members of Congress do not take responsibility for their votes against US national interests on behalf of Israel. After one such vote, some members came clean to the Washington Post about their feelings. "I displayed my usual cowardice," one House member said later, mocking his own vote for the bill that he had fought so hard against.[93]

[ii] This figure is the nominal sum of the deficit not adjusted for inflation.

Members of the United States business community were again stymied by the Bush Administration and Israel lobby's campaign to redirect American output toward one of the most inane causes ever conceived: the military invasion of Iraq. Foment for US military involvement against Israel's enemies had been on AIPAC's agenda for years. Ariel Sharon and the Israel lobby were on the record urging military action against Iran and Iraq even in March of 2001, months before the 9/11 attacks on America.[94] In some ways, the 9/11 attacks provided a powerful catalyst to once again misdirect the US economy at an advantageous moment for the Israel lobby. In May of 2001, leaders in the US business community were pushing for economic and political rapprochement with Iran, Libya, and Iraq through investment and deeper business relations, and they pressured the Bush administration to drop sanctions against those countries.[95] As late as October 2001, the US Chamber of Commerce was fighting to keep US policy from being co-opted by the Bush administration's neoconservative policymakers, the secret energy task force led by Dick Cheney, Israel lobby militarism, and problems with Iran that were primarily fabricated in Washington.

> London, Oct 25. The US Chamber of Commerce has called for the lifting of sanctions against Iran, saying they were counterproductive and causing the loss of at least US $3 billion in American business with Tehran.
>
> The business association, the largest in the world, also wants Washington to allow Iran's application to become a member of the World Trade Organisation (WTO) to be "considered fairly."
>
> The main problem with US policy is the "misconceptions some politicians have of Iran," the senior European representative of the US Chamber of Commerce, Peter-Hans Keilbach, told an international conference on "Investing in Iran" in London Wednesday.
>
> He said that the strongest business lobby in the US was putting pressure on Washington to "roll-back" the sanctions against Iran. American companies were losing "US $3 billion" a year from trade with Iran.
>
> Keilbach told some 200 delegates at the conference that he was convinced this figure "can grow even further" if the US government allowed American corporations to participate in Iran's development.
>
> He lamented that the events of September 11 did not act as a "wake-up" call for the Bush Administration to

identify some of the problems with US policy towards Iran, that were mainly in Washington.

An important initiative would be to get senior Iranian figures to attend the Chamber of Commerce's headquarters in Washington, Keilbach suggested, arguing that he "could have got visas."[96]

If the non-military industrial or energy players among US industries could choose between the two scenarios today, which would they pick? Achieving their spring and fall 2001 economic initiatives to open markets and dialogue in Iran, Libya, and Iraq, or being silenced by an administration and foreign lobby determined to support military intervention in Iraq under the false banners of "fighting 9/11 terrorists" and "weapons of mass destruction"? What if Iraqis were empowered to find their own solution to Saddam Hussein, a dictator who historically received vast US government support? If the clock could be turned back and the choices made in the broad interest of all Americans, the world might be a happier, wealthier, and more peaceful place.

Three: Election Law Violations

AIPAC has long asserted publicly that it does not direct support to US office seekers or violate US election laws prohibiting nonprofit corporations from supporting individual candidates. Evidence reveals that both assertions are demonstrably false. In particular, AIPAC affiliates and board members were caught rigging a California Senate race, as well as illegally coordinating political action committees to give favored candidates a winning edge. AIPAC regional director Murray Wood stated on the record that AIPAC never gave such support to candidates.

> Wood denied that any assistance was offered. That would be against AIPAC's longstanding policy, he said in a letter to the Los Angeles Times. He added that "We clearly did not offer, do not offer, and cannot offer financial or other assistance...not directly, not indirectly, not formal, not implied."[97]

Wood and another former AIPAC director, Michael Goland, would orchestrate a massive covert election fraud scheme designed to rig the outcome of the 1986 California Senate race and secure a win for Alan Cranston. Wood's blanket denials about illicit support for candidates would also be blown away when internal AIPAC memos were published showing that AIPAC directed and coordinated PACs.

AIPAC Directors Wood and Goland Rig the 1986 California Senate Race

California entrepreneur and real estate developer Michael R. Goland was a major player in targeting US political candidates on behalf of Israel in the 1980s. He made his reputation by mounting a massive campaign against Illinois Republican Senator Charles Percy. Coordinated Israel AstroTurf PAC contributions were also flowing to produce the Percy defeat. AstroTurf refers to deceptive groups, PACs, and other supposedly local grassroots coalitions that are actually fake. They are often created by corporations, including lobbying and public relations firms, to channel outside donations to local candidates. Goland took matters one step further with television advertisements paid for by fake campaign contributors:

> In 1984, Percy, chairman of the Senate Foreign Relations Committee, ran for re-election and was targeted for defeat

by the pro-Israel lobby for his support of the sale of AWACS radar planes to Saudi Arabia in 1981. Percy's opponent, Rep. Paul Simon, received $274,144 from the pro-Israeli PACs, more than any other Senate candidate in the 1983-84 period. But that equaled about one-quarter of the amount spent by Michael Goland, a California businessman and ardent supporter of Israel, who used more than $1 million of his own money to finance a stinging advertising campaign against Percy. Goland avoided campaign contribution limits by spending the money "independently," rather than at the direction of Simon. But Goland's money, which bought lots of anti-Percy advertising, was a major factor in Percy's defeat. The power flexed by the pro-Israel lobby was reminiscent of another Illinois race two years earlier when pro-Israel PACs pumped $104,325 into a successful effort to defeat Republican Rep. Paul Findley, who had represented the Springfield, Ill., area for 22 years.[98]

Goland, a former AIPAC board member,[99] leveraged his reputation in the Percy defeat as a "pit bull" for Israel hardliners in Congress. In the spring of 1985, Goland traveled to Washington, DC to meet with lawmakers and lobby against proposed arms sales to Saudi Arabia.

Goland was active again last spring on behalf of Israel, coming to Washington to oppose the Reagan administration's attempt to sell $3 billion worth of arms to Saudi Arabia. Just before the first Senate vote on the issue last May, Goland was taken to the Senate cloakroom by Sen. Rudy Boschwitz (R., Minn.) in an attempt to sway the votes of two Republicans who supported the administration's attempt. Boschwitz made it plain to his colleagues that this was the Michael Goland of "Percy factor" fame, a move that some senators and lobbyists felt constituted a crude form of intimidation.

Sen. Alan Simpson (R., Wyo.) later brought the incident up on the Senate floor, saying he was bothered by the notion that a legislator cannot waver in support of Israel and warning, "You cannot build friendship on threats or intimidation or talk of political retribution or the ancient political game of 'keeping score.'"[100]

A year later, Goland was working to reelect California Democratic Senator Alan Cranston by supporting a third-party "spoiler" candidate in the 1986 election. Goland and a number of associates and contributors who were "orthodox Jews highly supportive of Cranston and Israel"[101] supported the minor American Independent Party candidate Edward B. Vallen. Vallen stated to reporters that he was also offered financial support by AIPAC's regional director, Murray Wood in an effort to draw support away from Cranston's chief contender for the seat, Republican Congressman Edwin V.W. Zschau.[102] It did not matter to Wood or Goland that Vallen was also on record as stating bluntly that he "opposed Zionists."[103] The struggling third-party candidate's opposition to all things Israel did not dissuade Goland and his associates from supporting him as their "spoiler" candidate.

Goland's only goal was siphoning votes away from Ed Zschau to clear the way for a Cranston victory. To skirt federal campaign contribution limits, Goland and associates recruited 55 people to appear as the contributors to television ad spots for the American Independent Party candidate. The 55 human conduits were then reimbursed by Goland and his collaborators, the true donors, in violation of federal election law. [104]

The illegal stealth spoiler ploy worked. Vallen won 109,916 votes, approximately 5,000 more than Cranston's victory margin over Zschau. Goland's TV spots depicted Vallen as a "truer conservative" than Zschau, but also partially revealed Goland's covert spoiler strategy by stating that "Cranston and Vallen were the only men of integrity in the Senate race."[105]

On December 14, 1988, Goland was indicted on five counts along with Lyle R. Weisman of Beverly Hills and Sandor E. Habalow of West Los Angeles, for "conspiracy, making excessive contributions to a federal candidate, unlawfully making campaign contributions through conduits and causing false statements to be made to the Federal Election Commission." Goland filed a suit and later appealed the charges on free speech grounds, claiming that the First Amendment guaranteed his constitutional right to make unlimited anonymous contributions to candidates. The U.S. Court of Appeals for the Ninth Circuit affirmed the district court's decision to dismiss the suit and deny the appellant's motion to certify constitutional challenges to the Federal Election Campaign Act on May 21, 1990. The Federal Election Commission asserted that affirming Goland's claim would result in election chaos.

> The appeals court found no merit in this argument, observing that one purpose behind the disclosure provisions is "to keep the electorate fully informed of the sources of campaign funding....There is valuable information to be gained by knowing that Vallen took $120,000 from a Cranston supporter." Another purpose behind the Act's disclosure provisions is "to gather the data necessary to detect violations of the contribution limits." The court said that if Goland's position were adopted, one could avoid the contribution limits simply by making an anonymous contribution.[106]

Goland originally faced a maximum possible sentence of 17 years in prison and a fine of $1 million if convicted on all counts, while defendants Weisman and Habalow faced up to 16 years in prison and fines totaling $875,000.[107] Goland's first criminal trial ended on July 10, 1989 in a mistrial due to a hung jury. A federal grand jury then returned a superseding indictment with additional alleged violations of Federal Election Act contribution limits and of US criminal statutes on September 19, 1989. This second trial ended on May 3, 1990 with Goland's conviction on one misdemeanor count of making an excessive contribution. Goland was acquitted on four counts of conspiracy and making false statements. The jury deadlocked on the felony count of making false statements. [108]

Goland received a federal prison sentence of 90 days for the excessive contribution conviction on July 16, 1990. [109]

AIPAC spokespersons and Goland's defense attorney denied any AIPAC involvement in the election fraud case.[110] AIPAC would not publicly defend or comment on the actions of its former board member Goland or the involvement of regional director Murray Wood. However, the conviction and FEC action mattered little in Congress. In spite of the massive fraud, there would be no election "do-over," and Cranston retained his ill-gotten seat. The target of the secret campaign, Ed Zschau, initially commented on the indictments; he believed the drastic nature of the violations wouldn't change the election, but would at least bring large penalties and fines in the near future. Zschau's confidence was misplaced.

> "These after-the-fact prosecutions don't affect the outcome of the elections," he said. "But I think it's important to prosecute fully the election laws. People have to believe that if they violate the laws, they will get more than a small fine. I think that, if the charges are correct, Goland must have been thinking this was a risk worth taking."

> "It's very disappointing for a candidate and a campaign that works so hard so long to win an election to be defeated in a close race and find out later that an illegal tactic has been used."[111]

The lesson of the trial for AIPAC and other arms of the Israel lobby was that secret election law violations in key districts, even if investigated and indicted, would likely result in little more than misdemeanor-level penalties. AIPAC did not have to tip more than a few key elections to favored candidates to gain an aura of power in Washington. Massive sums spent on legal defense and novel claims of First Amendment rights challenging clear FEC statutes could be counted on to reframe the legal case in the court of public opinion and achieve sentences amounting to slaps on the wrist. The same powerful strategy of combining massive resources for legal defense and free speech appeals would reappear a quarter-century later in the espionage case of *USA v. Steven J. Rosen and Keith Weissman.*

The 1988 AIPAC AstroTurf Political Action Committee Coordination Scandal

AIPAC had long been suspected of creating and illegally coordinating political action committees (PACs) across the United States to elect or defeat US congressional candidates. Throughout the 1970s and early 1980s, AIPAC officials and supporters denied illegal coordination. AIPAC instead claimed that while politically active members wore many hats, they somehow maintained internal "firewalls" between their activities as political donors, grassroots lobbyists, American citizens, and "friends of Israel." This led to an uncanny pattern of campaign donations that AIPAC stated was not the result of coordination. Marvin Asher, one such activist, attempted to explain this to the *New York Times* in July of 1987.

> The committee's influence does not stop in Congress but carries over into election campaigns. Aipac officials say they stop short of endorsing candidates because they do not want to be perceived as having a public "hit list" for fear of alienating potential allies in Congress.
>
> Aipac officials do not purport to be able to deliver votes for a candidate and bristle at the suggestion of even a casual link between the committee and specific campaigns. They acknowledge that they are often called upon for advice about candidates, but say they provide such information as private citizens.
>
> "Very often I will specifically say, 'I am speaking to you as a private citizen,'" said Mr. Asher, a Chicago businessman who is treasurer of Citizens Concerned for the National Interest, a pro-Israel committee with no official ties to Aipac.[112]

Nevertheless, AIPAC simultaneously reveled in the widespread notion in Congress that it was directly responsible for, though could not be publicly linked to, the defeat of numerous prominent political candidates it branded as "enemies of Israel." Senator Charles Percy served in the Senate for Illinois until 1984. He was defeated as "anti-Israel" because he supported the sale of airborne radar planes (AWACs) to Saudi Arabia. Other prominent US politicians were targeted by AIPAC, such as Congressman Paul Findley, whose seminal book *They Dare Speak Out* focused public attention on

AIPAC's direct behind-the-scenes role in coordinating the defeat of independent-minded US politicians. The *New York Times* continued to explore AIPAC's connections to the Israel-focused PACs operating under neutral-sounding names that blossomed and spread across the United States. The notion that AIPAC officials and supporters could assume so many roles in their activities as foreign agents, lobbyists, and political operatives was gradually wearing thin, especially after AIPAC's senior and former senior officials became incontrovertibly tied to the political "hit lists."

> Perhaps the most obvious link between Aipac and fundraising is Mr. Amitay, the committee's executive director from 1974 to 1980. He later established and is now treasurer of the Washington Political Action Committee, the second largest pro-Israel PAC, which contributed $293,400 to Congressional candidates in 1985-86.
>
> Mr. Amitay is on Aipac's executive committee and communicates almost daily with the organization. He also publishes a newsletter that minces no words in praising some candidates and criticizing others.
>
> "Courageous Friend" Or "Negative Member"
>
> Reviewing Republican senators up for re-election in 1988, Mr. Amitay writes that Dave Durenberger of Minnesota has been a "courageous friend" and John Heinz of Pennsylvania a "down-the-line supporter," while Daniel J. Evans of Washington State has been the "most negative member of the Foreign Relations Committee" and Chic Hecht of Nevada "has disappointed many previous supporters in the Jewish community."
>
> Aipac members will be active in Presidential politics in 1987-88, but they have no coordinated strategy and no consensus on a candidate. [113]

AIPAC's public façade of assertions that it was not coordinating strategy or funds to political candidates was completely demolished in 1988, when the *Washington Post* published internal AIPAC memos revealing that AIPAC was highly active in illegally coordinating PAC disbursements to favored candidates.

AIPAC 1986 AstroTurf PAC Coordination Memo

(Source: Washington Post)

September 30, 1986

MEMORANDUM:

TO: KK

from: ES

RE: SEE ME

1. ICEPAC has done nothing in the CO, LA, & MO race. They have given $500 to Evans & Daschle - 6/30/86 they had 11,048. Try for 1,000 to Bond, Moore, Evans, Daschle, & Reid. *[handwritten annotations]* Call ASAP.

2. CT PAC did not get involved in LA. Gave $0 to Daschle & 1,000 to Evans as of 6/30/86.

3. YAP has done nothing for Evans & Daschle - WHY? 9/3/86

4. GEORGIA has not gotten involved in NV & MO and given 1,000 to Daschle. Try 1,000 Bond, 1,000 to Evans and 1,000 to Daschle. Evans, Daschle.

5. Congressional Action of Texas $8,162 has done nothing for Evans & Daschle NV & MO.
   Try $500 for Bond, Santini, Daschle & Evans

6. GOLD COAST has done nothing in NV or MO - Can you try $500 Bond, Santini, Evans & Daschle

7. Southern Florida Caucus - Try $500 Bond, Moore, Daschle, Evans

8. Five Towns - Try Santini, Bond, Moore

9. Kings PAC Try Moore

Internal AIPAC documents made available to the *Washington Post* revealed that the group's top political operative was actively involved in identifying which candidates to support, drafting appeal letters, and channeling money to several candidates in the 1986 Senate races.

A memo from Elizabeth A. Schrayer, then AIPAC's deputy political director, five weeks before that election urged an assistant to call several pro-Israel PACs and "try" to get $500 to $1,000 donations for five specific Senate candidates.

In the Sept. 30, 1986, memo, Schrayer listed nine pro-Israel PACs and noted that some had not contributed to certain candidates. For example, the memo said that one of the PACs, called ICEPAC, had given nothing to three candidates in whom she was interested. "Try for 1,000 to Bond, Moore, Evans, Daschle, & Reid. Call ASAP," Schrayer wrote, referring to Senate candidates Christopher S. (Kit) Bond (R) in Missouri, W. Henson Moore (R) in Louisiana, John V. Evans (D) in Idaho, Thomas A. Daschle (D) in South Dakota and Harry Reid (D) in Nevada. [114]

Contrary to AIPAC's public assertions, not only was it coordinating Israel PAC contributions, it was actively working to establish and fund more PACs in the mid-1980s.

Four other documents are 1985 letters from Schrayer to individuals in Massachusetts, California and Hawaii. In them, she offers to provide fund-raising ideas and arrange speakers for a new pro-Israel PAC, sends a sample solicitation letter and list of pro-Israel PACs to a fund-raiser for Evans, and volunteers to answer questions about starting a PAC.

...In addition to the Schrayer memo and letters, a "how to" booklet on setting up a pro-Israel PAC, dated February 1985, was available in Schrayer's office, according to a former AIPAC employee. [115]

AIPAC officials subsequently trotted out an oft-used cover story, saying that the fault lay with "unauthorized individuals and junior employees." This excuse was deployed rapidly in other cases when the press uncovered a juicy tidbit and a news story was breaking. AIPAC's defense also required public credulity toward the "internal ethical firewall" and believing AIPAC officials had acted forthrightly even as their "coincidental" activities appeared to have violated US election laws.

AIPAC officials have said, for example, that connections between the group and the growing number of pro-Israel PACs often headed by AIPAC members are coincidental. Thomas A. Dine, the group's executive director, was quoted as saying in 1985 that AIPAC was not a PAC, but an "information-gathering group. This organization doesn't touch political money."

Of the AIPAC members who headed pro-Israel PACs, he said, "I know them as activists. I don't know them as the head of a PAC."[116]

As AIPAC blamed "junior, now departed" staffers it was further revealed that these "junior staffers" not only tried to garner desperately needed publicity for the campaign of Richard A. Licht, but also attempted to plant stories about presidential candidate Jesse Jackson's sex life.

The brief response is in sharp contrast to the lengthy statement AIPAC issued last month following publicity about a November 1987 memo from a Schrayer assistant that urged an AIPAC spokeswoman to get reporters for Jewish newspapers to generate support for Richard A. Licht (D), a Jewish candidate who ran against Sen. John H. Chafee (R-R.I.) this fall, and to pursue allegations about Jesse L. Jackson's personal life and finances. That memo was denounced as the unauthorized work of a junior staffer. [117]

The American-Israel Public Affairs Committee, a pro-Israel lobbying group, Oct. 6 disavowed a year-old memo that had recently come to light. The memo urged Jewish reporters to raise questions about Jesse Jackson's sex life and finances. The memo also urged the "pro-Israel community" to support the challenge of Rhode Island Lt. Gov. Richard Licht (D), "who is Jewish," to Sen. John Chafee (R-R.I.), who was described as "a poor supporter of our issue." AIPAC did not make political contributions and had a policy of not endorsing specific candidates. Officials of the group said the memo was an unauthorized effort by a now-departed junior staffer.[118]

The bombshell *Washington Post* story and the internal AIPAC memos it featured were unequivocal. Based upon its examination of the AIPAC documents and applicable statutes, the *Post* bluntly declared that US election laws appeared to have been broken.

Federal law permits membership organizations such as AIPAC to communicate on a partisan basis with its members. The law also stipulates that political committees that establish, maintain, finance or control other committees are "affiliated" and thus subject to the contribution limits for one committee.

Over the past few years the number of pro-Israel PACs has grown dramatically. During the 1986 election cycle, for example, *The Wall Street Journal* compiled figures that 80 of these PACs donated nearly $7 million to candidates, sometimes more than $200,000 to a single candidate. This made them the most generous single-issue givers. A single PAC would be limited to giving $10,000 to a candidate in an election cycle.

Although AIPAC declined to answer questions raised by the Schrayer documents concerning its policy and legal positions in dealing with pro-Israel PACs, it made a statement to its employees last month. In the Oct. 21 edition of an internal newsletter, *The Macaroon*, AIPAC officials informed the staff of what they termed an upcoming political attack on the group's activities by CBS' "60 Minutes." [119]

The *Washington Post* made these assessments based on meticulous examination of the handwritten notes on the memos cross referenced to Israel PAC donations reported to the FEC. Compared to its coverage of the most recent AIPAC scandal—the indictments of two top-level officials in connection with violations of the 1917 Espionage Act—the *Post*'s earlier courage in confronting AIPAC wrongdoing is startling. The 1988 *Washington Post* story went on to assert the following:

Handwritten in the margin of Schrayer's Sept. 30, 1986, memo are notes that indicate someone at ICEPAC, one of the pro-Israel committees, was reached. The notes say the PAC gave $2,500 to Sen. Alan Cranston (D-Calif.)—a contribution confirmed by a check of the records—and that the unidentified ICEPAC representative would call back the next week when he had his "file with him" to discuss what appear to be "past and possible future" donations.

Dr. Morton Leibowitz of New York, ICEPAC's treasurer, said Friday that he does not remember any such call from anyone at AIPAC, although he keeps the PAC books in his office and signs the checks. He said he is a member of AIPAC, but not an active one.

FEC records show ICEPAC gave $3,500 to then-Rep. Daschle, $1,000 to then-Rep. Reid, and $500 to Evans, all Democrats, but nothing to former governor Bond of Missouri or then-Rep. Moore of Louisiana, both Republicans.

The Schrayer memo also noted that "Georgia has not gotten involved in NV & MO." It directed the assistant to "try 1,000 Bond, Evans, Daschle."

Handwritten notes say the PAC, known as Georgia Citizens for Good Government, had given an additional $1,000 to Evans and Daschle the month before, but also had supported Harriet Woods (D), who was opposing Bond in Missouri. The Georgia group gave another $2,000 each to Evans and Daschle on Oct. 8—after the Schrayer memo.

David Kuniansky, president of the Georgia PAC and an AIPAC member, said he knew Schrayer and her assistant but had never been called by either of them. "We [PAC members] don't listen to or are influenced by anyone but ourselves in deciding who to give to," he said.

The Schrayer letters made available to The Post date from early 1985. In a July 17, 1985, letter, Schrayer wrote to Morton L. Friedman, a Sacramento attorney, about Evans' race against Sen. Steve Symms (R-Idaho). She said that "as per our discussion," she was enclosing an Evans position paper on the Middle East, a "sample solicitation letter on behalf of John Evans to go to the pro-Israel PACs" and "a list of pro-Israel PACs to send the letter." She added: "I would suggest sending the letter out as soon as possible."

She noted that if Friedman had any questions, he could call AIPAC President Bob Asher in Chicago or one of her assistants.

Friedman agreed at first to answer questions about the Schrayer letter, but changed his mind. "I unfortunately can only speak off the record, even though I have very good responses to you regarding your inquiry. Unfortunately, I am subject to the policy of the organization [AIPAC] and cannot, therefore, respond even though I was not an officer in 1985," he said.

There have been other hints of an AIPAC role in partisan politics. During the 1986 campaign, a third-party candidate running against Cranston said he was offered financial support by AIPAC's regional director, Murray Wood, in an effort to draw support away from Cranston's chief foe, Rep. Edwin V.W. Zschau (R).

Wood denied that any assistance was offered. That would be against AIPAC's longstanding policy, he said in a letter to the *Los Angeles Times*. He added that "We clearly did not offer, do not offer, and cannot offer financial or other assistance...not directly, not indirectly, not formal, not implied."[120]

The publicity generated by the *60 Minutes* television segment drew letters to the editor alternately complaining about and praising the *Washington Post* exposé. Public attention soon turned toward the regulatory role of the Federal Election Commission and the question of its response to these stunning revelations. In what was already becoming an established and predictable pattern of ignoring law enforcement imperatives and leaving protest about AIPAC activities to outraged activists, the FEC signaled to the *Boston Globe* that it was not inclined to take any investigatory or enforcement actions.

Mike Wallace said in the report, "Under US federal election regulations, if it were shown that pro-Israel PACs were working in conjunction with AIPAC or were coordinated with AIPAC, that would arguably be a violation of the law."

However, an official at the Federal Election Commission told *The Boston Globe* the agency has no plans to pursue the case.

The commission can investigate potential violations in response to a complaint, or it can initiate its own probe.

The official said nobody had filed a complaint and, at least during the Reagan administration, the commission is not inclined to start investigations of its own accord.[121]

The FEC's decision not to investigate the allegations would not be the final word, as public outrage forced the issue into court.

FEC Sued to Enforce US Election Law over AIPAC Coordination

Interest in the emerging role of Israel lobby AstroTurf PACs operating across the US continued building well into 1989. Post-election reporting revealed that Israel PACs had donated a whopping $4 million to congressional candidates during the 1988 campaign. Three particular candidates received more than $200,000 from Israel PACs, while a handful of others had received in excess of $100,000, in a pattern of uncanny coordination in tight races.[122]

On January 12, 1989, a group of prominent former US government officials filed a complaint with the FEC over illegal AIPAC coordination, as reported in the *Sunday Oregonian*:

> In a complaint filed with the Federal Election Commission, a group of former U.S. government officials charged AIPAC with disregarding restrictions on lobbying by supplying money and volunteers to campaign for or against various political candidates based on their stand toward Israel.
>
> AIPAC, which was not a political action committee, was also accused of secretly coordinating the activities of as many as 53 smaller pro-Israel political action committees. The lobbying group labeled the allegations "totally absurd" and "harassment."
>
> Among the seven complainants were: George Ball, former undersecretary of state; James Akins, former ambassador to Saudi Arabia; Andrew Kilgore, former ambassador to Qatar; and former Representative Paul Findley (R, Illinois).
>
> The retired officials urged the FEC to force AIPAC and its many affiliated political action committees to register as a single political action committee, which would be limited by law to donating no more than $10,000 per year to each of those candidates it supported.[123]

The heart of their complaint was that the Federal Election Commission failed to require AIPAC to publish details of its income and expenditures, a legal requirement for political action committees. Richard Curtiss alleged "conspiracy and collusion," as reported by the Associated Press:

"AIPAC's formidable ability to mobilize congressional support...is based not upon an appeal to the American national interest but upon threats by a special interest that has resorted to conspiracy and collusion," said a statement by Richard Curtiss, formerly the chief inspector of the U.S. Information Agency and one of the plaintiffs...

If the charge of collusion is accepted by the FEC, it could find that the PACs exceeded their contribution limits because the law treats all contributions by affiliated committees as though they were made by a single group.

The complaint, which also demands that the FEC order candidates to return such excessive contributions, cited the 1988 Rhode Island senatorial race, which the complaint contends was targeted by AIPAC through its allegedly affiliated PACs.

Lt. Gov. Richard Licht, who was allegedly supported by $172,000 from pro-Israel PACs, ran against incumbent John Chafee, but lost. Chafee, who voted in 1981 to sell AWACS surveillance aircraft to Saudi Arabia, did not receive a dime from pro-Israel PACs, the complaint alleges.[124]

Additional complainants included Admiral Robert Hanks and Orin Parker, president of America-Middle East Educational and Training Services (AMIDEAST). The complainants had little reason to believe at the time that their legal effort would span almost two decades, rise to the US Supreme Court, and despite numerous appeals and amicus filings, never arrive at any definitive resolution of the core charges of illegal coordination detailed in the complaint. The filed petition contained more than 100 pages of exhibits alleging secret AIPAC PAC coordination and excessive contributions encompassing 53 Israeli PACs in the 1984, 1986, and 1988 election years.[125]

As the FEC began to reluctantly investigate the charges, it found AIPAC to be initially unwilling to cooperate or release documents.[126] AIPAC also stated publicly to the *Jerusalem Post*'s Wolf Blitzer that it appreciated the promised confidentiality of FEC proceedings and would studiously avoid information releases that would generate subsequent periodic news coverage.

"Realizing the potential for abuse, such as is found in this case, Congress deliberately provided for confidentiality in processing such matters before the FEC," the Aipac statement said. "Aipac will proceed under this provision as have virtually all other respondents in similar cases."

The FEC will eventually release the complete set of documents when the matter has been resolved. Aipac does not want to release its response, an Aipac source said, so that "there won't be a news story on the subject every two weeks..."

...In Jerusalem yesterday, the president of Aipac, Ed Levy, declined to comment on the allegations. (Levy is here as head of an Aipac delegation that is holding meetings with Israeli leaders.)

Levy said that a full response to the charges had been issued yesterday by Aipac headquarters in Washington. Members of the delegation felt that the organization would be vindicated in this affair, as it has been in similar investigations in the past.[127]

In the first live press events accompanying the complaint filing, Richard Curtiss outlined the operational details of PAC coordination and stealth by AIPAC:

As a retired foreign service officer and a long-term specialist on Middle East affairs, the question I'm most frequently asked is, why the American Israel Public Affairs Committee, which is registered to lobby Congress on behalf of Israel, is not also registered as the agent of a foreign power? The answer lies in AIPAC's claim that the bulk of its operating funds are received not from the government of Israel, but from groups of Jewish-Americans organized to support Israel. Therefore, although its policy is to provide all-out support to any democratically-elected government of Israel, AIPAC's directors maintain that technically they are not obliged to register as US agents of that government.

It appears to me, however, that in their relationships with the network of pro-Israel political action committees, AIPAC and its directors are violating the letter as well the spirit of US law. AIPAC provides the incentive and expertise to organize such PACs. Members and former members of its board of directors serve on the boards of many of these PACs. AIPAC designates preferred candidates in congressional elections all over the United States to guide the donations of these PACs. This guidance is very specific. It covers which candidates unfriendly to our issue, meaning Israel, are vulnerable and which candidates friendly to our issue need help. This guidance is actually issued in written form, as well as orally, and distributed to a restrictive circle of key PAC officers and major individual donors. It's knowledge of the existence of this AIPAC black book that generates congressional cooperation. The AIPAC clout is magnified by statements attributed to AIPAC staffers in the national network of Jewish weekly newspapers that the more than $4 million injected into each of the past three congressional elections by pro-Israel political actions committees is only the tip of the iceberg, representing 10 percent of total contributions poured into tight congressional races by pro-Israel individuals, all following AIPAC directions. The effort to make the source of AIPAC's clout clear to members of Congress is accompanied by an effort to hide its source from the general public. Of 91 pro-Israel PACs active in some or all of the past six years, no more than three or four make reference to Israel, Zionism, Judaism, or the Middle East in their titles. Their non-descriptive names, in fact, have become their hallmark. It makes them very easy to identify in the records of the Federal Elections Commission. This isn't just hearsay or media hype generated by AIPAC lobbyists to increase the perceived power of AIPAC. Evidence of collusion to coordinate and steer the donations of pro-Israel PACs abounds in the form of formal statements by AIPAC staffers, statements by AIPAC officers, and written internal AIPAC communications which have fallen into the hands of journalists. The results are also clearly documented in the listings of donations by these PACs filed with the Federal Elections Commission. Some 60 pro-Israel PACs had made donations in the 1988 congressional elections as of September 30th.[128]

Amid minimal press coverage, the FEC delivered its final report on the complaint on Friday, December 22, 1990. The report indicated that the PACs named in the complaint were no longer under investigation, but that some of the allegations against AIPAC itself were still being studied.[129] According to the *Washington Jewish Week*, the complaint forced AIPAC to alter its operations concerning PACs.

The complaint has changed the relationship between AIPAC and the PACs, according to one PAC official. Since the complaint was filed, he said, direct communication has ceased between AIPAC's political department and the PACs

"The need to respond to the complaint also forced AIPAC and the PACs to disclose a lot of information on the way they do business which now will be available to the public," he said.[130]

AIPAC was initially confident that it could continue with no further fallout from the "technical matters" raised in the complaint."

AIPAC general counsel David Ifshin said the decision "finally puts to rest the steady stream of unfounded allegations concerning AIPAC's legitimate activities. The remaining issue in the complaint is a technical matter AIPAC fully expects to be resolved in its favor. Any assertion to the contrary is wrong."[131]

However, the original team of complainants was not satisfied with the FEC decision. There was no documentation in the FEC's initial release or any findings or proposed actions against AIPAC. There was also no indication whether or not the entire investigation had been stymied by AIPAC's outright refusal to comply with the FEC's requests for internal financial records.[132] Time passed, and subsequent findings by the FEC proved less than adequate, if not galling to the complainants. The FEC then issued a written finding that AIPAC had made "in-kind donations" that "likely crossed the $1,000 threshold." This was the highest amount an individual or organization could then donate to a candidate seeking office in a single election. AIPAC therefore truly functioned as a "political committee" in the eyes of the FEC. However, in spite of the violation, the FEC ruled that it would not require AIPAC to register as a political action committee and disclose its donors and recipients, because organizing these types of campaign contributions was not "the major purpose of AIPAC."[133]

Supreme Court Ducks Complaint About AIPAC

Unsatisfied and angered, the original seven complainants filed a lawsuit in the Washington, DC Federal District Court against the FEC. In an August 12, 1992 press conference, the plaintiff's attorney, Abdeen Jabara, outlined the major unanswered concerns driving the lawsuit:

MR. JABARA: Good afternoon. My name is Abdeen
Jabara. I am one of the attorneys representing seven
plaintiffs in a suit that was filed this morning in the
Federal District Court for the District of Columbia, and
which has been assigned to Charles Ritchie. This lawsuit
brought on behalf of seven prominent American citizens
is against the Federal Election Committee (sic) and arises
out of a complaint that was filed by these seven
individuals more than three-and-a-half years ago. A very
detailed complaint which alleged among other things that
the American Israel Public Affairs Committee was in
violation of the Federal Election Campaign Act of 1971
in that—as well as 27 other political action committees
situated throughout the United States, pro-Israel political
action committees, in that they were affiliated with one
another and that they were organized and under the
control and direction of AIPAC. And therefore, the single
contribution limit of $5,000 per candidate for the primary
campaign for the candidate, and $5,000 limit for the
general election campaign of the candidate would apply
to all of the 27 PACs. Additionally, we allege that AIPAC
itself had made illegal corporate contributions to
candidates for political office, yet was not registered as a
political action committee. The Federal Election
Commission only after the bringing of a Mandamus
action in federal court, made the decision on June 16th of
this year, dismissing the complaint in terms of the
allegations of affiliation with the 27 PACs, finding that
AIPAC was not a political action committee, but finding
that it had made illegal corporate contributions to
candidates, but assessing no civil penalty therefore. The
plaintiffs in this action had 60 days in which to file a
complaint before federal district court in which they
allege basically three cause of action: that the Federal
Election Commission acted arbitrarily, capriciously, and
contrary to law in the dismissal of the administrative
complaint before the Commission, and that the Federal
Election Commission did not conduct a full, fair and
complete investigation of the administrative complaint
filed by these individuals. The complaint, a copy of
which is available here for your perusal, alleges that
AIPAC is incorporated as a tax-exempt lobbying
organization whose major goal is to enhance the US-
Israel relationship. And it lobbies the administration and
Congress on such items as maintaining the aid level to

Israel, which is the highest single recipient of American foreign aid. It maintains a political department which collects and makes available to AIPAC members and other pro-Israel PACs, information concerning current or upcoming campaigns for federal and other public offices. Among other things, the general counsel's office of the FEC in the conduct of its investigation found that there was evidence that members of the 27 PACs have served or were serving as AIPAC officers, that members of some of the respondent PACs had attended AIPAC's annual policy conference and received information on candidate's voting records on pro-Israel issues, and that there were similar patterns of contributions among some of the pro-Israeli PACs. It also found that AIPAC had sent out memoranda to various pro-Israel PACs, asking that the PACs donate money to named congressmen that were listed. In the administrative complaint that was filed before the Federal Election Commission three-and-a-half years ago, we attached an appendix of several hundred pages which includes computerized analyses of contribution patters, of interlocking, membership, leadership relationships in the PACs and AIPAC, et cetera, which in our estimation shows beyond any reasonable doubt that these PACs were operating indeed as one PAC, were affiliated. And indeed, AIPAC has admitted that it has held seminars around the country teaching people how to organize these PACs. And all of which, in our estimation, satisfies the requirement of control and direction under the law. In the 1986 general election, pro-Israeli PACs donated nearly $7 million to candidates, sometimes more than $200,000 to a single candidate. And officers of the pro-Israeli PACs often consult with AIPAC about candidates' voting records. And indeed, it was this steering of candidates to PACs by AIPAC which the Federal Election Commission found to be a providing of an in-kind service. Therefore, there are three causes of action under this complaint that was filed today in Federal District Court. One is the affiliation issue, the second is AIPAC as a political committee, and third is our complaint that the Federal Election Commission refused to levy civil sanctions, or civil fines against AIPAC for its violation of the law.[134]

Dick Mayberry also made a statement at the press conference decrying the lack of depositions and serious investigations of the PACs allegedly involved in coordination, while stressing that the FEC panel did find wrongdoing, but was not interested in punishing the perpetrators.

> MR. MAYBERRY: Good afternoon. My name is Dick Mayberry, a Washington lawyer. I specialize in federal election litigation. I am not going to repeat what Abdeen so eloquently stated in terms of what the underlying evidence is, what the charges are that were brought before the Federal Election Commission against AIPAC, the rejection of those charges by the Federal Election Commission, the need for our lawsuit to force the Federal Election Commission to make a decision on the underlying complaint after three and a half years, and now the instant lawsuit challenging the Federal Election Commission's throwing out of the complaint against AIPAC. Instead, I would like to supplement what he has said so well in comprehensively covering and giving an overview of what the situation is, and just make two or three points.
>
> First, the general counsel said that this case is largely made not on the evidence that was brought forward by the complainants, but that the answers in the information that was compelled from AIPAC when it was forced in the discovery process to answer interrogatories and produce documents, which in accordance to the investigative process of the Federal Election Commission it requires them to produce information. So the general counsel is making its report based on—largely on information provided by AIPAC. Now, it is our position, of course, that they did not go far enough. For example, we don't believe they took any depositions. And how you could investigate a case of this magnitude with 27 PACs and a major organization and not depose the chief executive officer of the organization or the chief political officer of the organization is—would defy all professional standards of conducting a plenary investigation. Consequently, we don't believe a complete investigation was undertaken.
>
> Nevertheless, with the investigation that was undertaken, the information was provided by AIPAC. And in it, AIPAC in—I would call your attention to the general counsel's report. You can get it at the Federal Election Commission. It is dated May 29th, 1992, and the Federal Election Commission is located at 999 E Street, Public

Records Office. And it summarizes the whole case. And basically, from the general counsel's position, it basically—this would be a good place to start because the record in this case is between three and four thousand pages long, and this document is 25 pages long. And in it, the general counsel states, AIPAC acknowledged that it routinely meets with candidates because they are candidates, and in addition to discussing the candidates' views on Middle East issues, also discusses campaign strategy and fundraising needs and goals with the candidates. In our view—that is the general counsel speaking— once AIPAC has held such meetings and held such discussions with a candidate, any subsequent activity or communication by AIPAC regarding that candidate with its so-called members would have to be viewed as communications undertaken in consultation with that candidate. This would constitute a campaign contribution. Since AIPAC is a corporation, and corporations are prohibited from making contributions, this would constitute an illegal corporate contribution, as Abdeen had stated.

Now, this is no small matter—37,000 members, they're canvassing most of the members of Congress. It takes tremendous resources, as we all know, in order to collect this information, distill it, and then distribute it in a form which is meaningful for use in terms of targeting funds and deciding which candidates to support and which candidates not to support.

On the basis of this, the general counsel recommended that the Federal Election Commission find probable cause to believe that AIPAC violated the law, one of the most serious provisions of the law, 441B—Title II, United States Code, Section 441B, Illegal Corporate Contributions, and that it be fined. The—this recommendation went to the Federal Election Commission, made of six commissioners—three Republicans and three Democrats. The commissioners found by a vote of four to two that there was probable cause to believe that AIPAC violated the law, however, that they would take no further action. In our opinion, we believe we have a strong case, because the amount of resources—one of the reasons given by the commissioners in terms of not sanctioning AIPAC was that it was a de minimis amount of resources or activities that I have just described. Well, of course, it couldn't be, because it's so expensive to undertake that activity in the scale that it was undertaken that it would appear that there is a very strong case in a situation in which a federal agency's own lawyers undertake an extensive three and a half year investigation, recommend a finding of violation of the law, recommend sanctions, and a commission turns around and finds no sanction—it finds a violation, but refuses to make the sanctions. Consequently, there—we go into federal court on this charge believing that we have a—that the conduct was clearly arbitrary and capricious, because if they violated the law, they ought to be punished. Period. Now, the last thing I want to close with is to tell you all, about four years ago—four and a half years ago, before this even started, I believe it was *60 Minutes* that had a program that revealed some of the information on AIPAC. And there's been this lawsuit now. There is a three- or four-thousand-page record at the FEC. There is now more information known in terms of the process of—let's treat it generically—of special interest groups influencing the political process now is known than perhaps has been known in many, many years. Because of the investigative process, AIPAC had to respond to interrogatories and document requests and had to file legal briefs and file answers. This can be produced, if you request, in the Public Records Office of the Federal Election Commission, a microfilm. And you can get—you can go through this very quickly, go to the general counsel's reports, start at the back and move forward. And I think what you'll find, you will find extremely illuminating information which would be worthy of study and consideration in terms of the actions of the Federal Election Commission and how it has handled this particular case. Thank you very much.[135]

The original seven complainants then went on to file a third appeal alleging that the FEC acted in bad faith dismissing the January, 1989 complaint against AIPAC, and that this faulty interpretation of the rules was not cause for exempting AIPAC from disclosing all details of fund receipts and expenditures.

The battle raged into 1995. In March, the DC Circuit Court of Appeals found two to one against the complainants. They then sought a hearing before the entire appeals court, and on May 8, 1996, eight justices ruled for the complainants and against the FEC, with two dissenting. The ruling identified a dangerous "slippery slope." Exempting a large and powerful organization like AIPAC from the rules concerning political activities on the grounds that such activities were not the organization's "major purpose" would facilitate abuse, as other organizations began to conduct large-scale political activities and candidate efforts with none of the FEC oversight, compliance and reporting required of political action committees.

In 1998, AIPAC intervened and appealed the Court of Appeals decision to the Supreme Court. On June 1, 1998, the Supremes decided that, in spite of AIPAC challenges, the complainants (referred to as "anti-Israel plaintiffs" by the *Forward*) did have "standing" to demand a resolution in court. However, the Supreme Court did not actually rule on the substance of the issue.

> Supremes on Aipac: The Supreme Court is telling the Federal Election Commission to reconsider the request of several anti-Israel plaintiffs for detailed information about the American Israel Public Affairs Committee. In a decision issued Monday and written by Justice Breyer, the court held that the plaintiffs have standing to ask the FEC for information about Aipac's membership and political contributions. The court did not rule on the substance of the matter: the question of whether Aipac is a political action committee. In a dissent, Justices Scalia, Thomas and O'Connor argued that the case should be tossed out and that the complaining former government officials lacked standing to sue the FEC. "The FEC should proceed to determine whether or not Aipac's expenditures qualify as 'membership communications,' and thereby fall outside the 'scope of expenditures' that could qualify it as a 'political committee,'" Justice Breyer wrote. An Aipac spokeswoman said, "We have no doubt the FEC will make it clear that Aipac is a membership organization, with complete freedom to communicate with its members on politics and elections."[136]

The US Supreme Court sent the case back down to the original US District Court. The surviving complainants (one has since passed away) continue to insist that whether or not AIPAC is a membership organization, as it claims, it is also a political committee required to disclose detailed donor and expenditure information to the public. **The case remains in limbo, almost 20 years after it began.**

The AIPAC Culture of Invincibility Grows

Some may wonder why an organization as successful at lobbying as AIPAC would take the risk of directly creating and coordinating PACs to influence elections. To AIPAC, there may have appeared to be little true risk involved, for two reasons.

The first is that the very creation of AIPAC was an audacious and ultimately successful exercise that bent the letter and spirit of at least two other laws—the Foreign Agents Registration Act and the Logan Act. Illegally creating and nurturing PACs in the United States in the 1980s was a relatively low-risk enterprise compared to Si Kenen's activities at AIPAC and its precursor lobbying and public relations organization, the American Zionist Committee. The American Zionist Committee didn't merely cross state lines: it crossed national borders. Funds weren't transferred from American donors to an obscure PAC conduit and on to a candidate, but from a distant foreign government entity, the Jewish Agency, via a conduit into Kenen's various US operations. Coordinating PACs was likely viewed from inside AIPAC as a logical progression of power building, and in comparison to Si Kenen's work, **a fairly low-risk operation.**

The second reason is that by the mid-to-late 1980s, no Fulbright remained on the scene in any branch of the US government positioned with a mandate to effectively question or check AIPAC's power. The general malaise extended to appointed bipartisan election law enforcement authorities at the FEC, who had little motivation or desire to investigate AIPAC. Even the Supreme Court lacked stomach: it ultimately never grappled with the core issues spelled out in the original 1988 FEC complaint. This visible institutional aversion to taking on AIPAC as a rogue corporation would later be repeated in the months leading up to the 2005 indictment of Keith Weissman and Steven Rosen for violating the 1917 Espionage Act.

A Rosen and Weissman defense memorandum detailed a Feb. 16, 2005 communication between Rosen's lawyer, Abbe Lowell, and Nathan Lewin, AIPAC's legal counsel. Lewin revealed that the U.S. attorney for the eastern district of Virginia and chief prosecutor in the case, Paul McNulty, "would like to end it with minimal damage to AIPAC." Lewin further told Lowell that US Attorney McNulty was "fighting with the FBI to limit the investigation to Steve Rosen and Keith Weissman and to avoid expanding it." [137]

Why McNulty fought so hard to restrict the scope of the FBI's investigation is perhaps less of a mystery than the retreat of the FEC and Supreme Court. Few know what transpired in the former US attorney's mind or private conversations in the final days before criminal indictments were handed down. What is known is that after discussing restricting the scope of the prosecution with AIPAC's lawyer and shortly after handing down indictments (August 4, 2005), McNulty was "kicked upstairs" by being nominated to the prestigious position of Deputy Attorney General on October 20, 2005. McNulty was sworn into office on March 17, 2006. It is perhaps both illustrative and ironic that a scandal surrounding alleged White House pressures on US attorneys to politicize their law enforcement priorities by pursuing dubious "voter fraud" prosecutions timed to swing elections led to McNulty's announced resignation. Scheduled to leave the DOJ in the summer of 2007 to join the law firm Baker and McKenzie,[138] McNulty was caught up in a larger web of deceit and accused of misleading Congress when he stated that US attorneys who refused to prosecute so-called "voter fraud" were actually fired for "performance-related" issues.

Four: AIPAC Power Expands

AIPAC's corporate entities in many ways reflect the American Zionist Council's departmentalized structure. Today tasks formerly performed by such units as the "Department of Information" are shared and tightly coordinated by AIPAC and affiliated think tank "scholars" as well as an expanded public relations contingent newly located on Madison Avenue. The former departments have grown into a network of separate nonprofit corporate entities, two declared as AIPAC affiliates and others that are not.

AIPAC currently operates as a nonprofit 501(c)(4) corporation. 26 U.S.C. § 501(c) is a provision of the United States Code providing for 28 distinct categories of nonprofits with varying levels of exemption from US federal taxes. Sections of the code from 503 through 505 list the requirements for attaining tax exemptions from the Internal Revenue Service. Many states accept Section 501(c) compliance to define which organizations are also exempt from state taxation.

Most exemptions are extended to nonprofit civic leagues and organizations operated exclusively for the promotion of social welfare, or local associations of local employees within a designated US municipality. Section 501(c)(4) exemptions are decidedly not intended to provide a legal cover to organizations exclusively promoting the interests of a foreign government from within the US. It can be argued that AIPAC violates the core 501(c)(4) principle that covered organizations exist to benefit social welfare within a designated US municipality. AIPAC's core purpose of securing aid, arms, and influence for a foreign country means that it should not qualify as a 501(c)(4) nonprofit. AIPAC's documented history of illegal activities should have led to the loss of its 501(c)(4) status from the IRS Tax-Exempt Organizations unit years ago, along with the dissolution of the corporation.

The net revenues of Section 501(c) organizations are intended to be devoted exclusively to demonstrable charitable, educational, and/or recreational purposes. Section 501(c)(4) organizations differ from 501(c)(3) in that they are permitted to lobby for legislation, but specifically not for candidates and generally not for foreign governments. Donations to 501(c)(4) organizations are not tax-deductible for donors. However the organizations themselves are not taxable entities and enjoy broad exemptions from corporate, excise, sales, property, and other taxes. The most widely recognized 501(c)(4)s organizations are dedicated to retiree interests, gun ownership, progressive politics, and environmental policies.

US Nonprofit 501(c)(4) Organizations

(Source: Internal Revenue Service Form 990 Filings)

501(c)(4)	Revenue (year)
American Association of Retired People	$797 million (2005)
National Rifle Association	$171 million (2004)
MoveOn.org	$6 million (2003)
League of Conservation Voters	$4 million (2005)

By law, all 501(c)(4) organizations must avoid any activity supporting or opposing individual US political candidates:

> ...no substantial part of the activities of which is carrying on propaganda, or otherwise attempting, to influence legislation (except as otherwise provided in subsection (h)), and which does not participate in, or intervene in (including the publishing or distributing of statements), any political campaign on behalf of (or in opposition to) any candidate for public office.[139]

As previously discussed, AIPAC's violations of this prohibition include establishing AIPAC-controlled stealth AstroTurf PACs, coordinating stealth AstroTurf PACs, laundering board member money in support of third-party candidates to influence elections, and conducting illegal television campaigns. If the laws governing 501(c)(4) candidate support were rigorously applied to AIPAC, it would no longer enjoy tax-exempt status.

If applied to AIPAC, another law governing US tax-exempt organizations and support for terrorism could cause it to lose its tax-exempt status:

> ...(i) the organization is designated or otherwise individually identified in or pursuant to such Executive order as supporting or engaging in terrorist activity (as defined in section 212(a)(3)(B) of the Immigration and Nationality Act) or supporting terrorism (as defined in section 140(d)(2) of the Foreign Relations Authorization Act, Fiscal Years 1988 and 1989); and (ii) such Executive order refers to this subsection.[140]

Israeli government officials were certainly involved in the Operation Susannah terrorist attack against US targets at the same time Jewish Agency executive and Finance Minister Levi Eshkol was channeling funds to the American Zionist Committee and AIPAC founder Si Kenen. Since AIPAC's beginning as the American Zionist Committee for Public Affairs, the group and its leadership have been strenuously engaged in garnering and channeling unconditional US political support for the ethnic cleansing and brutalization of indigenous Palestinian populations from conquered lands annexed, seized, or illegally occupied by Israel. The lobby's covert torpedoing of the Johnson plan as examined by Fulbright needlessly exposed the United States to decades of terrorist retaliation generated by brutal Israeli policies. The ongoing Israel lobby influence on US political debate and politicians has prevented the US from taking any role in negotiating a settlement of legitimate grievances generated by what the Arab world refers to as "*al Nakba*" (the tragedy). Indeed, AIPAC's leadership in the drive for the US invasion of Iraq has generated a new refugee crisis even larger than the Palestinian displacement caused by the creation of Israel.[141]

Even disregarding the Lavon Affair, a compelling argument can be made that AIPAC and affiliates could also be shut down immediately on the grounds that it is a leading, though indirect, generator of recent terrorist activity against the United States. The 9/11 Commission Report generally avoided deep analysis of the factors motivating the terrorist attacks on the United States. However, page 147 of the commission report does euphemistically refer to AIPAC driven policy as a core motive of Khalid Sheikh Mohammed, the so-called mastermind of the 9/11 attacks:

> KSM's animus toward the United States stemmed not from his experiences there as a student, but rather from his violent disagreement with U.S. foreign policy favoring Israel.[142]

Khalid Sheikh Mohammed's statement is appended by a reference note clarifying that his rationale for attacking the United States are the same as those of Ramzi Yousef, his nephew and the leader of the 1993 World Trade Center bombing. When Yousef was sentenced to a prison term of 240 years in 1998, he accused the United States of supporting Israeli terrorism against Palestinians, adding that he was "proud to fight any country that supports Israel."

AIPAC's lawbreaking in the interest of supporting the oppression of indigenous populations of the Middle East begets another crime: asymmetric retaliation against the United States. The line between AIPAC's corruption of the US political system and the aftermath of 9/11 has become a topic of concern for elite scholars at prestigious institutions that are normally reluctant to criticize Israel. John Mearsheimer is the Wendell Harrison Professor of Political Science at Chicago and the author of the book *The Tragedy of Great Power Politics*; Stephen Walt is the Robert and Renee Belfer Professor of International Affairs at the Kennedy School of Government at Harvard University. Mearsheimer and Walt provided clear analysis of the "unconditional support for Israel/terrorism against the US" linkage in their 2006 policy paper "The Israel Lobby":

Beginning in the 1990s, and even more after 9/11, US support has been justified by the claim that both states are threatened by terrorist groups originating in the Arab and Muslim world, and by "rogue states" that back these groups and seek weapons of mass destruction. This is taken to mean not only that Washington should give Israel a free hand in dealing with the Palestinians and not press it to make concessions until all Palestinian terrorists are imprisoned or dead, but that the US should go after countries like Iran and Syria. Israel is thus seen as a crucial ally in the war on terror, because its enemies are America's enemies. In fact, Israel is a liability in the war on terror and the broader effort to deal with rogue states.

"Terrorism" is not a single adversary, but a tactic employed by a wide array of political groups. The terrorist organisations that threaten Israel do not threaten the United States, except when it intervenes against them (as in Lebanon in 1982). Moreover, Palestinian terrorism is not random violence directed against Israel or "the West"; it is largely a response to Israel's prolonged campaign to colonise the West Bank and Gaza Strip.

More important, saying that Israel and the US are united by a shared terrorist threat has the causal relationship backwards: the US has a terrorism problem in good part because it is so closely allied with Israel, not the other way around. Support for Israel is not the only source of anti-American terrorism, but it is an important one, and it makes winning the war on terror more difficult. There is no question that many al-Qaida leaders, including Osama bin Laden, are motivated by Israel's presence in Jerusalem and the plight of the Palestinians. Unconditional support for Israel makes it easier for extremists to rally popular support and to attract recruits.[143]

AIPAC, the sharp tip of the Israel lobby spear, not only makes the US more vulnerable to terrorism—it continues to break US laws to do it. Organizational secrecy is AIPAC's key tactic for achieving success and avoiding potentially embarrassing disclosures of its real activities like those that occurred under Fulbright's oversight.

The AIPAC Culture of Secrecy

Throughout most of its history, AIPAC has been able to scoff at meaningful public disclosure while erecting an almost total veil of operational secrecy. This has protected AIPAC from press and regulatory scrutiny as its directors and operatives work behind the scenes to rig elections and lobby for policies against the US national interest. There is little doubt that the many instances of lawbreaking appearing in the press are but a fraction of AIPAC's total violations.

Secrecy has also protected big AIPAC donors from any financial backlash or consumer boycotts that might occur if word of their support were to leak out to pro-Palestinian or grassroots peace activists. Foot soldiers for more equitable regional policies might have given up Payless Shoes long ago if they had learned that the shoe store chain's founder was a major financial backer of AIPAC.[144] Since its founding, AIPAC has labored mightily and spared no expense (including Supreme Court appeals) to keep the identities of its donors a secret—even when found to be acting as a political action committee which by law is required to disclose this donor names and contributions.

Because of AIPAC's power, potential news sources and leakers are reluctant to discuss AIPAC on the record. Employees who leave AIPAC usually sign pledges of silence. AIPAC officials rarely give interviews, and the organization has historically refused to even divulge the names of its board of directors.[145] From time to time, the mainstream corporate media cautiously refers to this curious institutional culture of secrecy:

> "There is no question that we exert a policy impact, but working behind the scenes and taking care not to leave fingerprints, that impact is not always traceable to us (AIPAC)"—*The National Journal*[146]

> "Calculatedly Quiet"—*Fortune Magazine*[147].

> "Donor secrecy "—*LA Times*[148]

The press has faced two obstacles to reporting on AIPAC. The first is AIPAC's operational secrecy: even the basic information most nonprofits are eager to disclose to the public is routinely withheld by AIPAC. Second, as a *Nation* magazine reporter revealed, the press must overcome its internal resistance to digging out facts and airing AIPAC's dirty laundry for fear of reinforcing "stereotypes."

Why the blackout? For one thing, reporting on these groups is not easy. AIPAC's power makes potential sources reluctant to discuss the organization on the record, and employees who leave it usually sign pledges of silence. AIPAC officials themselves rarely give interviews, and the organization even resists divulging its board of directors. Journalists, meanwhile, are often loath to write about the influence of organized Jewry. Throughout the Arab world, the "Jewish lobby" is seen as the root of all evil in the Middle East, and many reporters and editors—especially Jewish ones—worry about feeding such stereotypes.[149]

This fear of "feeding stereotypes" is a powerful deterrent to warranted and critical press coverage. This complex fear means that if honest reporting uncovers too many negative facts, journalists generally put down their pencils and move on to other less dangerous subjects. Or, in other words, the crime is not the crime. **The crime is criticism, suspicion, or disapproval of AIPAC and the Israel lobby, however well founded and documented it may be. Self-censorship at such formerly courageous newspapers as the *Washington Post* and *New York Times* is now almost total, as a comparative review of AIPAC-related reporting from 1960 through the present day reveals.**

Concealing AIPAC's True Corporate Reach

Unfortunately for AIPAC and timid mainstream journalists, IRS disclosure requirements governing nonprofit corporations are becoming more strict, imposing transparency through yearly financial reporting mandates. Concerned citizens can consult lightly censored versions of AIPAC's IRS Form 990. The mandatory disclosure requirements of this annual nonprofit tax return covering revenues, expenses, and disclosure of board members, lobbying expenses, and related parties have increased in detail over the past few years. Although AIPAC (and other organizations) routinely file for extensions to report as late as possible, publicly available sections of yearly 990 filing data reveal robust growth in resources that AIPAC routinely refused to disclose in previous years.

AIPAC Reported Revenues, Expenses, and Net Assets (US $ million)
(Source: Internal Revenue Service Form 990 Filings[iii])

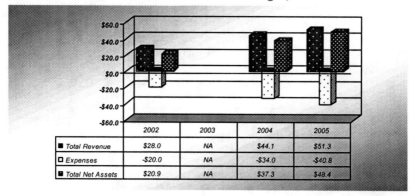

	2002	2003	2004	2005
■ Total Revenue	$28.0	NA	$44.1	$51.3
▢ Expenses	-$20.0	NA	-$34.0	-$40.8
■ Total Net Assets	$20.9	NA	$37.3	$48.4

When AIPAC's year 2006 IRS Form 990 is finally filed and made publicly available, AIPAC will probably confirm to the IRS and the public that it not only maintains significant office space in Israel, but also has signing authority over inscrutable offshore financial accounts. Alternatively, AIPAC may already have restructured itself in order to deny material linkages with both the offices and the untraceable offshore financial muscle through some new corporate structure aligned with evolving IRS form 990 requirements.

AIPAC publicly claims only a modest organizational reach, geographically and politically, and two related organizations. AIPAC's public tax filings portray an uncomplicated three-part affiliate organizational structure centered in Washington, DC. AIPAC is authorized to lobby Congress, but is not a registered foreign agent like the American Zionist Council. AIPAC registers as a domestic lobby. Near East Research (NER) is now a tax-exempt corporation that distributes Si Kenen's legacy newsletter with the support of tax-deductible donations. The American Israel Education Foundation (AIEF) is charged with taking members of Congress on "educational trips" to the "Middle East"—or more specifically, to Israel.

[iii] AIPAC's fiscal year is October 1 through September 30.

AIPAC: IRS-Disclosed Corporate Structure
(Source: Internal Revenue Service Form 990 Filings)

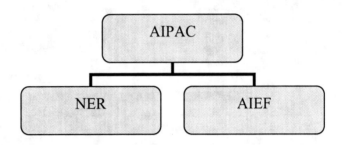

The American Israel Education Foundation, as the AIPAC arm now tasked with taking congressional representatives on Israel-centric "education missions," will also take staff, reporters, and other influencers. In the 1960s, organizations in the United States funded by the Jewish Agency began to lead organized tours for US opinion leaders, but had less success with members of Congress. Foreign financing for the trips came under fire at the Fulbright hearings in 1963, when it was revealed that a Jewish-Agency-funded organization called the American Christian Palestine Committee was heavily involved in "study trips" to Israel. Witness Gottlieb Hammer, the executive vice chairman of the Jewish Agency, unabashedly stated that the true purpose of the trips was to buy allies among influential Americans. While the lobby's objective has not changed, AIPAC's success in financing trips has improved to the point that members of the US Congress must now present credible and unassailable alibis for not making at least one trip to Israel.

Senator Fulbright: What was the purpose of the tour?
Hammer: To show these people conditions in the Middle East so that they would be better informed.
Senator Fulbright: Do you have any idea how many participated in it?
Hammer: No, sir....
Senator Fulbright: Why did the Jewish Agency finance these tours? What was the purpose of them?
Hammer: Specifically we were not asked to give approval for the tours. On the general program of inviting people who are leaders in their particular fields of

endeavor to visit Israel to see it firsthand was always regarded by the Jewish Agency as a worthwhile project. This is being done all the time, the idea or the thought being that if people who are influential in their own fields will visit Israel and see for themselves, that it is not necessary then to attempt to influence them. They will form their own judgments. **They may write articles or make speeches or do other things which will be helpful to the general problem of assisting the Jewish Agency in the job of generating a favorable climate and good public opinion for the work we do.**[iv]

Senator Fulbright: Was this expenditure reported in your reports to the Justice Department as part of your activities as a foreign agent?

Hammer. No, sir. Because this expenditure was included in the total amount which we paid to the American Zionist Council, which, in turn, was included in the total amount shown on the reports to the Justice Department under the designation of grants to affiliated organizations.[150]

The Jewish Agency's funding of these trips through the American Zionist Committee conduit in the 1960s in some ways resembles AIPAC's present use of the American Israel Education Foundation. However, instead of channeling Israeli government funds for trips, AIPAC directs tax-exempt donations to AIEF and then coordinates tax-advantaged "educational" trips to accomplish the very same objectives—except that now, these trips are almost exclusively extended to US lawmakers. AIPAC is not the only lobby playing this game on Capitol Hill, though it does dominate the field in terms of total sponsored trips to Israel. Congress has expressed little interest in rectifying lobby-driven travel conflicts of interest, even after numerous scandals involving tax-exempt funding for congressional "fact-finding" trips.

The American Israel Education Foundation

Congressional trips to Israel sponsored by the American Israel Education Foundation are often defined as "junkets" designed to secure the undivided attention of legislators while isolating them from broader regional realities. They are promoted as educational events, but former Senator James Abourezk found the trips to be largely propaganda efforts designed to push or fortify the Israeli government line with US legislators:

> According to the Jewish *Daily Forward* newspaper, congressional filings show Israel as the top foreign destination for privately sponsored trips. Nearly 10 percent of overseas congressional trips taken between 2000 and 2005 were to Israel. Most are paid for by the American Israel Education Foundation, a sister

---

[iv] Author's emphasis.

organization of the American Israel Public Affairs Committee, the major pro-Israel lobby group.

These trips are defended as "educational." In reality, as I know from my many colleagues in the House and Senate who participated in them, they offer Israeli propagandists an opportunity to expose members of Congress to only their side of the story. The Israeli narrative of how the nation was created, and Israeli justifications for its brutal policies omit important truths about the Israeli takeover and occupation of the Palestinian territories.[151]

Analysis reveals a gap between the stated nonprofit mandate of the AIEF and its observable activity.

American Israel Education Foundation: Mandate vs. Activity

(Source: IRS 990 Filing, IRmep)

Near East Research IRS Nonprofit Mandate	*Observable Activities*
...maintain and further the understanding of the issues affecting relations between the United States and Israel through information and education provided to public and private parties interested in such relations. AIEF sponsors a wide range of in-depth study missions to Israel that allow members of Congress, Capitol Hill staff, reporters, and students to see firsthand the challenges facing the Jewish State. Recent trips have included missions specially designed for Spanish-language media professionals and another for non-Jewish student leaders.	Deliver tailored Israeli government propaganda to members of Congress, pundits, and the media elite, emphasizing Israel's positioning as a victim of regional events and an ally to the US. Minimize congressional visitor contact and productive relations with Israel's regional rivals. Encourage members to go on trips to Israel as a public and constituent display of commitment and fealty.

Congressional ethics rules prohibit members from taking trips paid for by registered lobbyists. However, by coordinating these trips under the auspices of the American Israel Education Foundation, AIPAC helps members skirt these ethics rules. This subterfuge also allows tax-favored treatment for the donations that are gathered and coordinated to pay for trip-related expenses such as airfare and lodging. Through AIPAC's efforts, Israel has become a startlingly popular destination for members of Congress.

Congressional Trips to Israel: 1/1/2000-6/30/2005

(Source: Center for Public Integrity "Power Trips" Database)

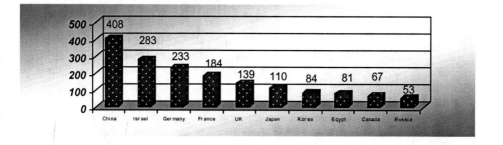

Members of Congress traveled to Israel 283 times on sponsored trips from January 1, 2000 through June 30, 2005, according to the Center for Public Integrity's database of trip filings. The Center for Public Integrity scoured physical copies of disclosure forms, many incomplete or illegible, at the Senate Office of Public Records, located on the second floor of the Hart Senate Office Building. House travel forms are physically stored in the House Legislative Resource Center in the basement of the Cannon House Office Building. At the time of the study, no online or digital public access to filings was available.

AIPAC's affiliate, the American Israel Education Foundation, sponsored 184 of the trips, most of which were filed as "educational" and "fact-finding" missions. The only other destination receiving so much congressional attention was China (408 visits). However, the sponsors of China trips were a more diverse mix of trade-oriented and economic-development-oriented entities. Israel was a unique destination because of the fact that 65% of trip sponsorships came from a single lobby's adjunct foundation, the American Israel Education Foundation.[152]

Si Kenen's Enduring Legacy: The *Near East Report*

The other AIPAC-acknowledged affiliate is a nonprofit corporation called Near East Research, Inc, which continues to publish Si Kenen's newsletter, the *Near East Report*. Near East Research publishes this thinly disguised Israeli government propaganda after modifying and massaging it into the mandatory AIPAC doctrinal mold that "US and Israeli interests are identical." Si Kenen created the *Near East Report* in June of 1957. Kenen emphasized the independence of the *Near East Report* and the separation between the newsletter and AIPAC in a letter to Senator Fulbright in 1963:

The Near East Report is not an organ of the American

Israel Public Affairs Committee. The committee purchases the Near East Report for all Members of Congress (as reported in its lobbying return), for some editors who have expressed a desire to receive it, and for contributors who earmark part of their contributions for that purpose. [153]

Since that time, the *Near East Report* has dropped any pretense that it is anything but an "organ of the American Israel Public Affairs Committee." There is no evidence that the publication and distribution of the *Near East Report* is still funded by donations from the Jewish Agency or payments from the Israeli consulate, [154] as was the case during the 1950s and 60s. However, the content of this bombastic and widely read propaganda invariably emphasizes contrived themes of Israel's right to "self-defense" through geographic expansion, the Middle East within improbable contexts of the European Holocaust, and the postulate of united US-Israeli military action against global "Islamic terrorism." Historically selective and blinkered, the *Near East Report* has little to say about the legacy and broad embrace of terrorism as the preferred tactic of many of Israel's founders, the brutal ethnic cleansing of Palestinians in the years prior to Israel's independence, or other important issues affecting the actual regional balance of powers, such as Israel's longstanding covert nuclear weapons program.

Highlighted text box excerpts from recent issues of the *Near East Report* reveal the heavy handed bombast with which Israeli concerns are unabashedly represented as America's own:

"Israel Has Ceded 93 Percent Of The Territory It Won While Defending Itself During The Six-Day War In Return For Peace Treaties With Arab States It Fought In 1967." *Near East Report*, June 1, 2007

"The Notion That Something Terrible Could Happen Here [In The Weeks Before The Sixday War] Was So Deeply Felt That Israelis Again Started Talking About The Holocaust." *Near East Report,* May 15, 2007

"As The Challenges To Israel And To U.S. Support For Israel Increase, It's Important To Have A Broader Base Of Support For The State Of Israel In America." *Near East Report,* February 5, 2007

"A Recent Agreement To Expand U.S-Israel Homeland Security Ties Was 'A Breakthrough, A Landmark In The History Of The U.S.-Israel Relationship.'" *Near East Report,* February 19, 2007

"Palestinian Terrorists In The Gaza Strip Are Trying To Turn The Area Into An Armed Stronghold Reminiscent Of Hizballah's Former Base In Southern Lebanon." *Near East Report,* April 30, 2007

The *Near East Report*'s frothy rhetoric tailors Israeli government spin into talking points and digestible sound bites which can be heard repeated by many US policymakers, mainstream media pundits, and other influential individuals who, like Senator Fulbright, receive their subsidized copies of the newsletter every fortnight. While few objective or respected Middle East scholars give the *Near East Report* high marks for accuracy, comprehensiveness, or even historical relevance, since it is so highly selective in choosing and framing issues, the newsletter provides red meat to AIPAC's legions of supporters and fellow-travelers who either have decided to toe the Israeli line for political reasons or don't wish to be armed with a more comprehensive and complex set of facts and perspectives on the Middle East. The *Near East Report* is referenced as a source primarily by think tank books on the Middle East and opinion magazines such as *Commentary,* rather than by publications from major universities or academic study centers.[155] Near East Research's activities also differ widely from the nonprofit's IRS mandate.

Near East Research: Mandate vs. Activity

(Source: IRS 990 Filing, IRmep)

Near East Research IRS Nonprofit Mandate	Observable Activities
Near East Research, Inc, is a nonprofit organization established to advance the research and study of people and nations of the near east through conferences, newsletters and other publications.	Israeli government propaganda, positioning Israel's regional rivals as enemies of the US and urging the application of US resources, including tax dollars and military might, toward Israeli objectives.

Near East Research's corporate structure as a 501(c)(3) organization means that any outside individual donations it receives are tax-deductible. This propaganda newsletter formerly subsidized by the Israeli government, has achieved the status of required reading at top-tier corporate media outlets as well as in the halls of Congress. It is now subsidized by all US taxpayers through tax breaks and the tax-deductibility of contributions and tax-exempt corporate operations. The academic quality of the publication is seldom raised among avid readers. The legacy of the *Near East Report*'s founder, Si Kenen, who was not an academically recognized expert on the Middle East, lives on at the newsletter. **An overwhelming commitment to Israel, rather than to academic rigor, international legal frameworks, or a comprehensive**

historical approach to the Middle East, continues to drive *Near East Report* content. However, reviewing only the activities of AIPAC's declared affiliates does not present a complete picture of the organization today.

How Big Is AIPAC Now?

The corporate structure AIPAC officially declares in IRS filings is much smaller than can be observed after examining AIPAC's geographical presence and history of direct and indirect AstroTurf PAC coordination. AIPAC has regional offices across the US as well as one in Jerusalem. Control extends down to AIPAC from links with Israeli government officials and informal links with major organizations such as the World Zionist Organization and AIPAC's original backer, the Jewish Agency. AIPAC's observable influence, in turn, cascades down to AstroTurf political action committees at the state level and operatives in every congressional district. Even this snapshot of AIPAC is truncated by excluding AIPAC alumni who continue to pursue the organization's objectives from positions as interns in congressional offices, within the Department of Defense and US State Department, in corporate America, and especially in the elite corporate media. One notable media perch is the CNN "situation room."

AIPAC: Observable Organization

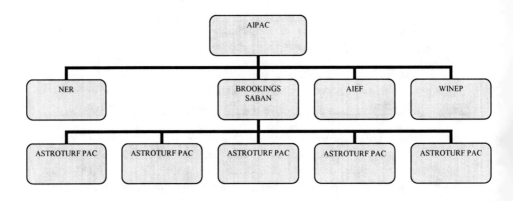

AIPAC manages its public relations operations close to the epicenter of the advertising world in New York City, where it occupies space at 477 Madison Avenue in Manhattan.

Situated on the corner of 51st Street and Madison Avenue, the 23-story property is in the heart of Midtown Manhattan. "The building is a small, well-run 1950s vintage office building with an excellent tenant roster, stable ownership and an outstanding location," David Hoffman, executive managing director of Colliers ABR, told CPN.[156]

AIPAC signed a ten-year lease in 2005 for 15,063 square feet, the entire 11th floor of the building, which serves as its' northeast regional office.[157] In Washington, DC, AIPAC occupies space close to Farragut Square at 440 1st ST NW, Suite 600, while the American Israel Education Foundation facility resides on the floor above (Suite 700). Near East Research occupies space within the same AIPAC suite at 440 1st ST NW (#600). The Washington Institute for Near East Policy is 2.5 miles across town from AIPAC, near Capitol Hill and Senate office buildings at 1828 L St NW. WINEP is also less than nine minutes travel time from National Public Radio headquarters on Massachusetts Avenue, where WINEP analysts appear frequently as "objective experts" on nationally syndicated programs such as *All Things Considered* and *Morning Edition.*

The Washington Institute for Near East Policy

Martin Indyk, an Australian national and naturalized US citizen was the former deputy director of research at the American Israel Public Affairs Committee. Indyk helped establish the Washington Institute for Near East Policy in 1984 with the support of AIPAC board member and activist Barbi Weinberg. Weinberg "had for over a decade privately wrestled with the idea of creating a foreign policy center." [158] After the establishment of WINEP, Indyk stated that he was still dissatisfied and wished to establish an institution capable of escaping AIPAC's reputation as a "strongly biased organization."[159] Indyk would later go on to found the Saban Center for Middle East Policy at the Brookings Institution. The center was initially funded by a $13 million grant from Israeli dual citizen and television magnate Haim Saban,[160] famously quoted by the *New York Times* as saying, "I'm a one-issue guy and my issue is Israel."[161] He also funded and established the Saban Institute for the Study of the American Political System within the University of Tel Aviv.[162]

WINEP's role within the AIPAC power constellation is clear. While AIPAC lobbies with brute force for yearly aid allocations and enforces adherence to Israeli doctrine in Congress, WINEP polishes and shines Israeli policy objectives as pure expressions of US foreign policy interests. AIPAC is secretive about its internal deliberations and activities, but the highly sociable WINEP cultivates the image of a serious group of objective "scholars and wonks" deliberating Middle East policies in a rigorously academic fashion. WINEP not only hosts symposiums and conferences, but also conducts closed-door meetings with US politicians and distributes books and other publications rich in toned-down AIPAC ideology.

While AIPAC officials are loath to do live media events, especially with call-in or other potentially interactive audience segments, WINEP analysts and authors are omnipresent across major news- and policy-oriented programs. However, media announcements rarely mention WINEP's overlap with AIPAC and other members of the Israel lobby or its close connections to Israel, although this would provide listeners and viewers with useful context for understanding the organization's sophisticated positions. WINEP is also a place for grooming future presidential appointees, and it is perceived as a less controversial and more credible stepping stone to power than AIPAC.

Although AIPAC does not list WINEP as an affiliate in its IRS filings, in 2004 26% of AIPAC's board of directors were also trustees of WINEP.[163]

WINEP's ability to place stories that sway American public opinion toward supporting Israeli objectives is quantitatively revealed by analyzing the number of print media stories developed from WINEP content and analysts over a period of five critical years. Access, rather than merit or quality of content, drives WINEP's news media success, according to former Middle East Studies Association President Joel Beinin:

> While Aipac targets Congress through the massive election campaign contributions that it coordinates and directs, Winep concentrates on influencing the media and the executive branch. To this purpose it offers weekly lunches with guest speakers, written policy briefs, and "expert" guests for radio and television talk shows. Its director for policy and planning, Robert Satloff; its deputy director, Patrick Clawson; its senior fellow, Michael Eisenstadt, and other associates appear regularly on radio and television. **Winep views prevail in two weekly news magazines, *US News and World Report* and *The New Republic* (whose editors-in-chief, Mortimer Zuckerman and Martin Peretz, sit on Winep's board of advisers).** The views of Winep's Israeli associates, among them journalists Hirsh Goodman, David Makovsky, Ze'ev Schiff and Ehud Ya'ari, are spoon-fed to the American media.[164]

An analysis of major print coverage of WINEP-attributed content between the years 2001 and 2006 reveals that WINEP is not always engaged in a full-on media blitz. Rather, its media power is exercised cyclically as initiatives are strategically "brought to market." In 2002, WINEP went on the offensive, tying the 9/11 terrorist attacks on the US to Israel's own efforts to subdue Palestinians and making a broad and vitriolic call for a greater US military role in the Middle East. Using the ProQuest print media database citations as an index, WINEP boosted war messaging media placements by 7%. In 2002-2003, AIPAC went into overdrive, secretly working Congress to support the ill-fated invasion of Iraq based on "weapons of mass destruction" and other pretexts. WINEP "analysts" began an all-out media blitz to "substantiate pretexts" and urge a hasty US military invasion of Iraq in the face of global opposition. Dennis Ross, the ubiquitous director of WINEP, eloquently appealed for public rejection of containment and other measures short of immediate US military invasion in a typical *Baltimore Sun* op-ed on March 13, 2003:

> Sooner or later, Mr. Hussein, with nukes, would miscalculate again, making the unthinkable in the Middle East all too likely.
>
> Some might reasonably argue that there are better ways to ensure he does not acquire nuclear weapons. Enhanced containment, with open-ended and intrusive inspections, could prevent Mr. Hussein from acquiring or developing these weapons. True, but is such a regime realistic? When the Bush administration came to power, the existing containment regime was fraying.
>
> The alternative of war has made France a convert to enhanced containment for the time being. It has also provided Mr. Hussein an incentive to grudgingly, and always at the last minute, take the minimal steps required to keep us at bay.
>
> Does anyone believe that in the absence of more than 200,000 U.S. troops in the area Mr. Hussein would be taking even his minimal steps? How long would he continue to "cooperate" if the troops weren't there? How long would the French insist on intrusive inspections if we weren't on the brink of war? And how long can we keep such a large military presence in the area?
>
> The unfortunate truth is that we cannot maintain a war footing indefinitely. The paradox is that our large-scale military presence creates the potential to contain Iraq, but it is sustainable neither from our standpoint nor from the standpoint of the region. Either we will use it to disarm Mr. Hussein or we will within the next few months have to withdraw it. And once we began to remove it, several new and dangerous realities would emerge.[165]

The WINEP media placement index reveals a jump from 611 to 672 between the year 2002 and 2003—a 10% increase in mainly Iraq-invasion-focused media placements.

WINEP Media Placement Index

(Source: ProQuest Print Database Search)

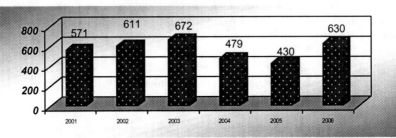

In the post-invasion fallout after public discovery that weapons of mass destruction were not the imminent threat to the US that had been portrayed by WINEP and many other operatives, WINEP saw no need to maintain a "surge"-level media blitz. The mission of getting US troops into Iraq, mirroring Israel's own occupation of Palestinian territories, had been accomplished.

However, the post-invasion index jump from 430 to 630 indicates that WINEP is again on a mission. It is no secret that the new military objective is Israel's arch-nemesis, Iran. **Although the US public is vastly more skeptical about the claims of war partisans, the 47% increase in Iran-centric WINEP media placements should be understood as a leading indicator of military conflict in 2008 if WINEP and AIPAC meet their objectives.** Given the elite status and political muscle of WINEP trustees, the efforts of AIPAC's think tank should not be underestimated, especially in an election year. WINEP meets before the entry of a new president to debate and draft the administration's Middle East "blueprint." Many WINEP trustees believe that this policy mandate affecting all Americans is the prerogative of its handpicked commission members, including officials of the Israeli military establishment. Brian Whitaker of *The Guardian* questioned whether any other foreign principal could accomplish the same maneuver.

> The Washington Institute is considered the most influential of the Middle East think tanks, and the one that the state department takes most seriously. Its director is the former US diplomat, Dennis Ross.

> Besides publishing books and placing newspaper articles, the institute has a number of other activities that for legal

purposes do not constitute lobbying, since this would change its tax status.

It holds lunches and seminars, typically about three times a week, where ideas are exchanged and political networking takes place. It has also given testimony to congressional committees nine times in the last five years.

Every four years, it convenes a "bipartisan blue-ribbon commission" known as the Presidential study group, which presents a blueprint for Middle East policy to the newly-elected president.

The institute makes no secret of its extensive links with Israel, which currently include the presence of two scholars from the Israeli armed forces.

Israel is an ally and the connection is so well known that officials and politicians take it into account when dealing with the institute. But it would surely be a different matter if the ally concerned were a country such as Egypt, Pakistan or Saudi Arabia.[166]

AIPAC's influence in the US news media leads to curious and generally unnoticed subsidiary alumni reunions. On June 14, 2007, following a Hamas takeover of Palestinian installations in Gaza, Wolf Blitzer invited Dennis Ross into the CNN situation room to give his perspective on the instability. Customarily, Dennis Ross's new book and WINEP affiliation were mentioned; AIPAC and the pervasive Israel connection were not. Equally unmentioned were Wolf Blitzer's former career as a reporter and editor of the *Near East Report* in the 1970s and his authorship of a comprehensive apologia downplaying the damage caused to the US by Jonathan Pollard's spying for Israel in his book *Territory of Lies.*[167]

Although WINEP's media influence is growing, compared to other think tanks, AIPAC's ability to place public policy messages in the news media through WINEP was comparatively limited until 2002. Thanks to a timely "acquisition," AIPAC and WINEP can now count on broader promulgation of AIPAC policy ideas through the Brookings Institution, one of the oldest and most highly regarded public policy think tanks in the United States.

The Saban Center for Middle East Policy

Brookings Institution Middle East policy research was placed under the direction of former AIPAC deputy director for research Martin Indyk in May of 2002. In an Internet video presenting the Saban Center, Indyk vastly understates both Haim Saban's biography and his contribution to Brookings by referring to it as merely the "generosity of a Los Angeles businessman." In 2006, *Forbes* magazine more accurately described Saban as the 98th richest person in America and the "Egyptian-born, Israeli-raised, now-American cartoon king."[168] Indyk does not, however, understate how assembling hand-picked researchers to produce tightly messaged policy research can be thought of as "a business" in his Saban Center introductory video.

> Haim Saban, a, uh, businessman in Los Angeles, came to Brookings with a desire to see us do more work on the Middle East issue. On the issues of the peace process, and terrorism, and the spread of weapons of mass destruction, and energy issues. And, uh, was prepared to put up the funds to get the center started. Through Haim Saban's generosity, we are now able to launch a much larger effort to promote innovative policies, research and analysis that brings together the best minds in the business.[169]

It is useful to carry Indyk's "business" analogy a bit further. In 2003, Haim Saban led the $5.7 billion purchase of Kirch Media Group; in 2001, News Corporation and Saban sold Fox Family Worldwide for $5.1 billion. Saban was part of an investor group that won the bid for Univisión, the biggest Spanish-language media corporation in the United States, in June of 2006. Financially speaking, Saban's $13 million Brookings investment secured control over one of the most financially robust as well as influential policy think tanks. In 2005, the Brookings Institution's net assets totaled $269,660,363.[170] From Saban's perspective as a savvy media player concerned with promoting the policies of Israel's government, taking over Brookings Middle East policy by launching the Saban Center in 2002[171] was yet another sound and extremely timely business investment—this time, in the marketplace of ideas. According to 2002 research by media watchdog Fairness and Accuracy in Reporting, Brookings led think tanks in total US media influence, measured by the number of policy analyst and report citations appearing in major US media.

Think Tank Share: US Marketplace of Policy Ideas

(Source: Fairness and Accuracy in Reporting)

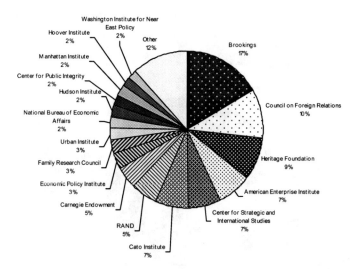

By targeting and taking over Middle East policy at Brookings in 2002, Saban and Indyk were able to "leapfrog" AIPAC messaging from second to last in the think tank market (WINEP had only 2%) to first place. Taking over Brookings also made it appear to Americans that there was now an "expert consensus" from "right to left" on the key Middle East policy issue of the year: the US invasion of Iraq on weapons of mass destruction pretexts. Brookings is often portrayed as a "centrist to left think tank" in the corporate news media. According to FAIR, "Progressive or Left-Leaning" media citations were a small but important segment of the marketplace of ideas, but combined with "centrist," they represented the majority. For Saban and Indyk, taking over Brookings Middle East policy in 2002 meant penetrating the 63% of the marketplace of ideas that was generally not beating a drum for war in Iraq.

US Think Tank Policy by Political Ideology
(Source: Fairness and Accuracy in Reporting)

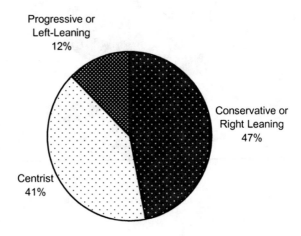

Progressive or
Left-Leaning
12%

Conservative or
Right Leaning
47%

Centrist
41%

The arguments in favor of the Iraq invasion in the many Saban Center articles appearing across major newspapers, such as "Lock and Load" by Martin Indyk and Kenneth M. Pollack, Director of Research at Saban, did not differ in message from those of AIPAC's own Washington Institute for Near East Policy and Dennis Ross. It would have been odd if they did, since, like Indyk, Kenneth Pollack worked at WINEP as a "research fellow" specializing on Iraq. [172]

> Rather, the Bush administration could take the time it needs to "study" the Iraqi declaration, discussing its falsehoods and fabrications with allied governments until it has lined up all the necessary political and military ducks. Once the best case has been made and the preparations completed (probably in a few weeks), President Bush could announce that, in accordance with United Nations Resolution 1441, we and our allies have concluded that Iraq is in material breach of the 1991

cease-fire resolution and therefore the U.S. will lead a coalition to disarm Iraq by force.

If there must be war, this is the best way. The problem with allowing the inspections to play themselves out is that it is a policy based on hope, and as Secretary of State Colin Powell is fond of saying, "hope is not a plan...."

There is real risk in allowing the inspections to run on indefinitely. The longer the inspections go on and find nothing, the harder it will be for the U.S. to build a coalition when we finally decide to take action.[173]

The takeover of Brookings Middle East policy by an AIPAC operative and Israeli-American businessman represents an evolution in AIPAC influence over think tanks. From a business perspective, AIPAC has moved from "investment in startups" to "establishing subsidiaries" to the more recent stage of "corporate takeovers and acquisitions." AIPAC has evolved strategically as a result of success and failure. Financing Dr. Benjamin Shwadran's highly academic policy research at the Council on Middle East Affairs with Jewish Agency funding laundered through the Rabinowitz Foundation was problematic and nearly crumbled under the glare of Fulbright's 1963 Senate probe. Even setting up the Washington Institute for Near East Policy in 1984 with AIPAC donor funds and board member involvement still did not give AIPAC the desired influence level of other less "captive" think tanks, particularly in the US news media. The takeover of Middle East policy at Brookings achieved what AIPAC had long sought in the marketplace of public policy: prestige, ideological spectrum dominance, and the highest level of achievable corporate media placement for its public policy initiatives. The American people are now more susceptible than ever before to AIPAC's "weapons of mass destruction" propaganda campaigns and other targeted media messages emanating from its right, left, and center public policy "think tanks." AIPAC and Saban are apparently convinced that the same messages can be effectively rebranded and simultaneously broadcast from both WINEP and Brookings. "Lock and Load" co-author Kenneth Pollack proved this during media appearances on CNN and Fox News in which he was successfully positioned as a liberal Bush Iraq war critic gradually coming to see the wisdom of the US military occupation, as documented by news watchdog *Media Matters*:

During the July 30 edition of CNN Newsroom, anchor Heidi Collins introduced Kenneth Pollack of The Brookings Institution by saying that Pollack "has been a vocal critic of the administration's handling of the [Iraq] war, but he says that an eight-day visit has changed his outlook a bit." Collins also said that Pollack's "tune is changing a bit" with respect to the war. Pollack went on to discuss how a recent visit to Iraq has left him "more optimistic" about the war. However, while focusing on Pollack's criticisms of the "handling" of the war, Collins failed to note that Pollack was an influential proponent of the Iraq invasion before it happened, leaving viewers with the impression that Pollack was a war opponent who has become more supportive of the war. Pollack's 2002 book on the subject was titled *The Threatening Storm: The Case for Invading Iraq.*[174]

Saban and AIPAC can be confident that few of the message's target viewing population knew about Pollack's record or key financial backer. They can also count on a new generation of eager AIPAC activists to populate think tanks and congressional offices in coming years thanks to "Saban Training" at AIPAC.

This summer GDI is proud to send two of its members to the American Israel Public Affairs Committee (AIPAC), Saban Training. On July 22, Joshua Sussman and Jen Sovronsky will travel to Washington, DC for 4 days of intense advocacy training.

The Saban conference is AIPAC's premier student political leadership training seminar, presented through its Schusterman Advocacy Institute, is held twice each year in Washington, D.C. More than three hundred of AIPAC's top student activists from over 100 campuses participate in three days of intense grassroots political and advocacy training. During this seminar, students meet with top Washington policy makers, elected officials, and Middle East experts.[175]

However, even as Saban advocacy training and activities continue in Washington, the potentially explosive outcome of a criminal trial across the Potomac in the Eastern District Court of Virginia could change the way many Americans view AIPAC.

Five: AIPAC on Trial

On August 27, 2004, CBS News broke a story about an FBI investigation into an Israeli spy network in the US Department of Defense. The initial press reports indicated that the FBI had uncovered a spy in Undersecretary of Defense for Policy Douglas Feith's office, working as an Iran policy analyst. Feith, who directly reported to Deputy Secretary of Defense Paul Wolfowitz, resigned under a cloud of suspicion in January of 2005. The spy for Israel was later identified as Colonel Lawrence Franklin, who had previously worked as an attaché at the US embassy in Israel. Franklin and one other mid-level Pentagon official in the office of the Secretary of Defense were responsible for Iran policy in the office's "Northern Gulf Directorate." Two high-ranking AIPAC officials were snared in the counterespionage dragnet, and their story has not yet fully unfolded or even gone to trial.

A major legal battle has been raging behind closed doors for almost two years, unbeknownst to most Americans due to a pronounced lack of serious media coverage.[v] The original scandal was well documented by mainstream news sources, although the first leaks to CBS News may have been for all the wrong reasons, as such leaks often are. Subsequent mainstream coverage of the trial of AIPAC officials have largely served to bolster the defense team's case without examining the public interest angles. Big media has also made a formal legal foray into the trial on the AIPAC defendants' behalf.

Colonel Lawrence Franklin Sentenced

Colonel Franklin was indicted along with two high-level employees of AIPAC; he later pled guilty to passing a classified Presidential Directive and other sensitive documents concerning US Iran policy to AIPAC. AIPAC officials then passed the information to Israel and select members of elite media in an attempt to influence the US's policy. The *Washington Post* somewhat minimized the fact that the investigation was initiated in 1999 in an article titled "Leak Probe More Than 2 Years Old":

> The investigation of Franklin is coincidental to the
> broader FBI counterintelligence probe, which was already

---

[v] Some of the following content and IRmep analysis has appeared previously in a series of articles about the legal case published by the Randolph Bourne Institute's news website, Antiwar.com.

long underway when Franklin came to the attention of investigators, U.S. officials and sources said.[176]

Some bloggers and online media pundits sympathetic to the Israel lobby claimed to have evidence that the case was actually "on the verge of fizzling out" when the news story of the counterintelligence investigation broke. However, the fast-breaking stories that the investigation had been launched four years earlier led to speculation by other non-mainstream analysts that the publicity of the case may in fact have been a "controlled burn." In this case, the burn was alleged to have stymied a successful counterintelligence investigation against Israel that went much higher and wider than Lawrence Franklin. A plausible "controlled burn" analysis for the media leak was made by the libertarian Antiwar.com editor Justin Raimondo:

> ...no source is given for this information, which runs counter to the mainstream reporting that this was, as Laura Rozen put it, a "controlled burn." Investigators were caught flat-footed by the CBS report, and were forced to move quickly to interview suspects—and there is speculation that the Israeli contacts they were most interested in apprehending were alerted to the danger, and took the opportunity to flee the country.[177]

Lawrence Franklin pled guilty to three conspiracy counts on October 5, 2005. Franklin revealed that his actions were a result of frustration and professional aspirations to secure a more influential position in the Bush administration, to be brokered by AIPAC. His frustrations about the lack of harsher, more military-oriented U.S. policies toward Iran were shared by AIPAC officials Steven J. Rosen and Keith Weissman. Franklin met with them regularly in 2002 and later passed information he knew to be classified with the hope that it would help the AIPAC lobbyists promote a more militaristic approach to Iran. He also asked Steven Rosen to use his influence to get him a job on the president's National Security Council. Rosen told him, "I'll see what I can do," according to Franklin.[178] Franklin also passed other classified information to an Israeli official concerning military activities in Iraq and weapons testing in Arab countries. Franklin admitted that he knew some of the documents he passed along could be used to the detriment of U.S. national security interests, a clear violation of one provision of the 1917 Espionage Act.

On January 20, 2006, Judge T.S. Ellis, III sentenced Franklin to 12 years and 7 months in prison and a $10,000 fine for passing classified information to AIPAC and the Israeli diplomat. The Israeli foreign ministry would later confirm that the diplomat who met with Franklin was Naor Gilon, publicly known as the head of the political department at the Israeli Embassy in Washington and a "specialist" on Iran's alleged nuclear weapons program. It is not known whether this was simply Gilon's diplomatic cover for Mossad agency activities. Upon learning of the investigation, Gilon initially fled to Israel to prepare a defense, only to return to the United States later in 2005.

The indictments of only Franklin, Rosen, and Weissman may mean that the "controlled burn" worked. The Pentagon was relieved that only a relatively low-level official was indicted and released a statement to that effect: "The investigation involves a single individual at DOD at the desk officer level, who was not in a position to have significant influence over U.S. policy."[179]

However, this official statement ignores later revelations that Douglas Feith's Office of Special Plans had deployed Larry Franklin for sensitive projects involving foreign contacts and overseas travel, including a meeting with Iran-Contra provocateurs. It remains a mystery that Feith was even in such a sensitive Pentagon position; in 1983, Feith had been fired from the National Security Council on allegations of passing classified documents to the Israeli embassy in Washington, DC.[180] Franklin was principally a "gopher" for more powerful figures in the neoconservative movement, such as Feith— none of whom were indicted, according to Professor Juan Cole, Franklin:

> ... moved over to the Pentagon from DIA, where he became the Iran expert, working for Bill Luti and Undersecretary of Defense for Planning, Douglas Feith. He was the "go to" person on Iran for Deputy Secretary of Defense Paul Wolfowitz, and for Feith. This situation is pretty tragic, since Franklin is not a real Iranist. His main brief appears to have been to find ways to push a policy of overthrowing its government (apparently once Iraq had been taken care of). This project has been pushed by the shadowy eminence grise, Michael Ledeen, for many years, and Franklin coordinated with Ledeen in some way. Franklin was also close to Harold Rhode, a long-time Middle East specialist in the Defense Department who has cultivated far right pro-Likud cronies for many years, more or less establishing a cell within the Department of Defense.[181]

And according to the British newspaper *The Guardian*, Feith's office had an unconventional relationship with Israel's intelligence services and hard-line right-wing Likud party members:

> The OSP was an open and largely unfiltered conduit to the White House not only for the Iraqi opposition. It also forged close ties to a parallel, ad hoc intelligence operation inside Ariel Sharon's office in Israel specifically to bypass Mossad and provide the Bush

administration with more alarmist reports on Saddam's Iraq than Mossad was prepared to authorise.

"None of the Israelis who came were cleared into the Pentagon through normal channels," said one source familiar with the visits. Instead, they were waved in on Mr. Feith's authority without having to fill in the usual forms.

The exchange of information continued a long-standing relationship Mr. Feith and other Washington neo-conservatives had with Israel's Likud party.[182]

Rosen and Weissman had good reason to believe that they, like Feith, would never face any consequences for their alleged illegal activities on behalf of Israel. The defense team worked hard to have the case against them dismissed during pre-trial motions—one aided by changes to Department of Justice prosecution guidelines made by the very US attorney who originally indicted them.

Rosen and Weissman Pre-Trial Dismissal Gambits

According to the indictment, although Lawrence Franklin walked into an ongoing FBI investigation out of the blue, the FBI had Rosen and Weissman under surveillance since the spring of 1999. Not only was the FBI tapping their telephone lines and following them to numerous meetings, mostly in Washington, DC, but it appeared that the AIPAC lobbyists were actively taking countermeasures to avoid detection. In one instance in 2003, the men hopped from "one restaurant to another" in Union Station before finishing their meeting.

The FBI did not move on AIPAC's headquarters until long after the investigation's cover had been blown. On December 1, 2004, FBI agents raided the Washington, DC offices of AIPAC and seized computer equipment and files from Executive Director Howard Kohr, Managing Director Richard Fishman, Communication Director Renee Rothstein, and Research Director Raphael Danziger. Ultimately, the FBI did result in charges against any of them, and not much is publicly known about the seized evidence.

Rosen and Weissman were charged with violating provisions of the 1917 Espionage Act. The robust defense mounted by their team of elite lawyers almost succeeded in getting charges dropped on narrow technicalities. In pre-trial legal maneuvering, Judge T.S. Ellis considered defense team motions on everything from the tangibility of the classified information being passed to novel First Amendment assertions reminiscent of Michael Goland's election fraud trial claims. He also strictly followed the criminal indictment by requiring government prosecutors to prove the defendants were guilty of passing information that could be used both to the injury of the United States **and** to the advantage of a foreign nation. The 1917 Espionage Act only specifies that defendants be guilty of injury **or** advantage. Defense team challenges forced Judge Ellis to reschedule every officially announced trial date in 2006 and 2007. At the time of this book's publication, the trial was set to begin in early 2008. [183]

In a March 2006 hearing, the defense team concentrated on portraying the 1917 Espionage Act as fundamentally flawed and unconstitutional. The indictment charges Rosen and Weissman with violating sections of the Act by having "unlawful possession" of "information relating to the national defense." Originally written in 1917, the Espionage Act does not use the term "classified" when referring to national defense information. The law's musty antiquity offered the defendants abundant openings for attack, which they brilliantly exploited.

The mainstream corporate media came to the aid of Rosen and Weissman by promulgating the defense team's "slippery slope" argument. The *Washington Post* argued more than once that the charges leveled against two foreign lobbyists could soon be turned against investigative journalists:

> The case has drawn attention from First Amendment lawyers because the judge, the prosecutors, and the defense attorneys have all noted that the two lobbyists, in receiving and disseminating classified information, are doing what journalists, academics, and experts at think tanks do every day. [184]

Ironically, this "issue frame" was adopted and repeated by staff reporter Walter Pincus, the same investigator who had helped assemble evidence of foreign agent influence for Senator Fulbright in 1962. The original reporting by Pincus that motivated the Fulbright investigation was broadly focused on ten lobbying groups, including Israel, active in the US. Pincus plausibly explains his focus on the free speech aspects of the Rosen and Weissman case as a function of his job as a top national security reporter and his legal background:

> I took up the Rosen-Weissman case because I was involved, by which I mean subpoenaed, in both the Libby and Wen Ho Lee cases. And with a recent law degree (J.D. Georgetown Law School 2001) have a personal interest in First Amendment and common law privilege involving the press and others, including lobbyists and students of foreign policy...
>
> The issue I looked at most closely is the question of just what is classified—and in the AIPAC case it is material

delivered orally with only the vaguest notion that the person delivering it says it is CIA or classified, or whatever. I get told that every day by sources and thus under the argument in the Rosen-Weissman case I am violating the Espionage Act every time I hear someone say that—or am I?

In short, there is no connection between what AIPAC stands for and advocates and my coverage of that court case.[185]

The *Washington Post* and other groups of elite reporters no longer explore "what AIPAC stands for." In the 1980s, AIPAC had to defend itself against *Washington Post* investigative journalism and fallout from publication of its internal memos. Now *Post* reporters are eager partners and recipients of "deep background" tidbits and stolen classified data doled out by AIPAC. Curiously, even erroneous reporting tends to benefit defendants in the trial. Pincus has written many additional criticisms of the Rosen and Weissman prosecution that have been of great public relations value to the defense team. One in particular contained a minute but significant error understating the breadth of the Espionage Act statute that was later propagated by other reporters. Pincus fought the *Washington Post* ombudsman for a month before allowing a correction to be issued, as we detail later.

Scores of other news outlets have written articles advancing the "think tanks and lobbyists do it every day" sentiment about classified information leaks. But would cracking down on think tanks and lobbies trafficking classified information be such as negative thing? It is possible that shutting down illicit conduits for classified information could actually benefit the majority of Americans who live outside the Beltway. The elite mainstream US press, specialty outlets such as the Jewish Telegraphic Agency, and many Israel-centric Middle East think tanks continue to spend great amounts of time scouring the branches of government for recruits willing to release highly sensitive classified information that ultimately finds its way to Israel. Many think tanks such as WINEP, functioning as stealth lobbies, seek an unfair advantage and influence through their access to classified information, just like Franklin, Weissman, and Rosen are alleged to have done. Taking away the motivation to seek and leverage classified information could function as a kind of policy "Regulation Fair Disclosure," or "FD." Regulation FD is an important rule governing stock trading in the securities industry. In this case of classified information, small stakeholders in U.S. policymaking, rather than small investors, would be less easily outmaneuvered by "inside traders" like AIPAC. However, this aspect of the case has not received any traction in mainstream reporting. The *Washington Post*'s days as an AIPAC watchdog eager to publish damning internal documents or groundbreaking exposés are long over.

The Weissman-Rosen defense has also sought to throw out the indictment on a number of other technicalities, including allegations that since no physical documents were passed, only verbal information, no crime was committed. The most novel defense claim, asserted by attorney Abbe Lowell, advanced AIPAC's own postulate that facilitating the trafficking of classified national defense information from the Pentagon to Israel via lobbyists could be anything but beneficial to the United States. In breaking the law, Rosen and Weissman are charged with passing information that "could be used to the injury of the United States or to the advantage of any foreign nation."

> There's a disjunctive, your Honor. The disjunctive says "injure the United States or assist or benefit the advantage of a foreign country." How can anybody apply that in a context in which good foreign policy for the United States, that clearly is intended to help make the United States' foreign policy better, may also have a derivative impact that makes it an advantage to an ally of the United States, *whose interests are exactly the same?* [186]

This assertion put forth by the defendants and AIPAC may prove to be their core weakness if they attempt to present it at their upcoming criminal trial. While Congress may have no problem with it, real outside experts could finally be called to testify in a truly relevant forum in order to inform the court that Israeli and US interests are often diametrically opposed. There is ample empirical evidence to prove this and the documented subterfuges of the Israel lobby beyond any reasonable doubt. The myth that Israeli and US interests are exactly the same is an elaborate ruse that could finally be debunked and terminated through expert testimony at the invitation of the prosecution team.

Intangibles and Fifth Amendment Rights

An August 9, 2006, opinion by presiding Judge T.S. Ellis III dealt a decisive blow to the defense team's efforts to achieve the full dismissal of the case on the basis that allegedly trafficked classified information was "intangible." The government's case against Rosen and Weissman hinges on applying the Espionage Act, which states,

> [W]hoever, lawfully or unlawfully having possession of, access to, control over, or being entrusted with any document, writing, code book, signal book, sketch, photograph, photographic negative, blue print, plan, map, model, instrument, appliance, or note relating to the national defense, willfully communicates or transmits or

attempts to communicate or transmit the same to any person not entitled to receive it, or willfully retains the same and fails to deliver it on demand to the officer or employee of the United States entitled to receive it ... shall be punished by a fine of not more than $10,000, or by imprisonment for not more than two years, or both.

Rosen and Weissman's request for dismissal based on intangibility was a complex challenge to the application of the Espionage Act. The defendants stated that oral transmissions of national security information cannot be prosecuted, since they are intangible. They also argued that national security information itself is improperly defined by US legal statute. Judge Ellis swatted down the esoteric hairsplitting through a combination of dictionary definitions and citations of legal precedents clearly revealing that national defense information is extremely well defined and can be transmitted orally:

Indeed, this conclusion is buttressed by a statement of the district court in Morrison,[vi] in which it stated that the statute – defines all types of tangibles: "any document, writing, code book, signal book, sketch, photograph, photographic negative, blueprint, plan, map, model, instrument, appliance, or note relating to the national defense," and also describes intangibles: "information relating to the national defense which information the possessor has reason to believe could be used to the injury of the United States or to the advantage of any foreign nation."[187]

The defendants had also mounted a constitutional challenge to the Espionage Act based on the principle that the "due process" clause of the Fifth Amendment prevents punishment pursuant to a statute so vague that "men of common intelligence must necessarily guess at its meaning and differ as to its application."

Judge Ellis's opinion on Rosen and Weissman's request for dismissal based on this gambit left no doubt about who is and who is not entitled to receive classified national defense information. Citing precedent and the

---

[vi] United States v. Morrison is a 1988 case frequently cited as precedent to arguments about leaks of classified information to reporters. In the case, the defendant stated that because he leaked classified national defense information to a news media outlet rather than a foreign power, he was not spying or subject to US law protecting classified information. The court rejected this argument, stating that the language of statutes against trafficking national defense information covers "anyone."

government's classification protocols, which Rosen was aware of after receiving his own security clearance for his previous work at RAND,[188] the Ellis opinion clarified that Rosen and Weissman were located far outside the circle of those entitled to receive national defense information.

The Ellis opinion also reiterated that trafficking only orally transmitted classified information, which is "intangible" and cannot bear written "secret" stamps, would not absolve Weissman and Rosen. The opinion held that if the government could prove the two knew they retransmitted closely held information with "a bad purpose either to disobey or to disregard the law," they would be found guilty.

FBI transcript snippets from the original indictment reveal that this may be a difficult obstacle for the defendants to overcome in trial. On June 11, 1999, Weissman allegedly told an Israeli government official that he had obtained a "secret FBI, classified FBI report."

Rosen and Weissman's defensive dodge that the indictment violated their First Amendment free speech rights was similarly knocked out in the opinion. Judge Ellis was lenient in granting that a First Amendment review would be warranted even for operatives trafficking classified data as a specific function of their lobbying efforts:

> [E]ven under a more precise description of the conduct—
> the passing of government secrets relating to the national
> defense to those not entitled to receive them in an attempt
> to influence United States foreign policy.[189]

However, precedent intervened again. Ellis found numerous cases of First Amendment rights being superseded by the specific details of the activity in question, obligations to protect national security, and the conduct of communication:

> ...with respect to the First Amendment, "the character of
> every act depends on the circumstances in which it was
> done."[190]

On a more superficial level, the judge's willingness to toss out the defendants' challenge is tied to the opinion's detailed description of the circumstances of one meeting with a Pentagon official, Lawrence Franklin, who was already convicted of passing information to the AIPAC operatives.

> In August 2002, Rosen was introduced to Franklin
> through a contact at the DoD. The two agreed to meet on
> August 21, 2002, but the meeting was postponed. Rosen,
> Weissman, Franklin and another DoD employee finally
> met nearly six months later, on February 12, 2003. At this
> meeting, Franklin disclosed to Rosen and Weissman

information relating to a classified draft internal United States government policy document concerning a certain Middle Eastern country. He told Rosen and Weissman that he had prepared a separate document based on the draft policy document. The three alleged co-conspirators met again on March 10, 2003 at Union Station in Washington, D.C. The three men conducted the meeting in successive restaurants and ended the meeting in an empty restaurant.[191]

Walter Pincus of the *Washington Post* continued to churn out stories repeating the defense team's claims of First Amendment rights to national security information. Pincus came to Rosen and Weissman's defense again with a deceptive story about the breadth of the 1917 Espionage Act. On March 24, 2006, the *Washington Post* was forced to issue the following correction to the Pincus story after a lengthy process between the paper's ombudsman and the Institute for Research: Middle Eastern Policy (IRmep).

A March 24 article said the Espionage Act makes it illegal for an unauthorized person to receive or transmit classified information that the person believes could be used to the injury of the United States **and to** the advantage of any foreign nation. The language of the 1917 law actually says the information could be used either to the injury of the United States **or to** the advantage of a foreign nation, but it need not be both.[192]

Pincus vigorously resisted issuing a correction during the ombudsman process and suggested instead that the complainant "take his argument to the prosecutors."[193] However, the ombudsman consulted an outside expert who found that the Pincus error was material and that the newspaper had to issue a correction. The fact that the 1917 Espionage Act does not require only intent to create "injury of the United States," since classified information is often trafficked and sold by third parties to other more hostile third parties, is a fact lost on many members of the mainstream press, including the *Washington Times*, which repeated the Pincus error without correction. Similarly esoteric issues continued to be hashed out in the pre-trial motions. While Pincus claims he writes about the AIPAC espionage case from the perspective of a news producer with concerns about freedom of speech, another *Washington Post* reporter admitted he served more as AIPAC's "conduit" than a reporter concerned with the mundane interests of news consumers.

Thomas W. Lippman spent nearly two decades writing about US policy as the *Washington Post*'s Middle East bureau chief and national security correspondent. When asked in mid-2007 to respond to an early account of the Rosen and Weissman criminal trial within the historic context of AIPAC operations, Lippman responded that he could not separate his personal relationship and gratitude for unsourced "background" information supplied to him by the defendants.

> Weissman and Rosen were confidential sources and I consider them friends. I also consider the criminal case against them to be unfair. [194]

A review of two decades of Lippman's Middle East reporting reveals little relevant or penetrating analysis about how US regional policy is formed. It does reveal a lot of headlines that look as though they could have been written by AIPAC, such as "Clinton Lacks Economic Leverage over Israel in Settlements Dispute." The public interest in knowing how policy is truly made has clearly fallen by the wayside. Lippman and his former newspaper can no longer be counted on to write detached analytical stories about AIPAC and Middle East policy. Lippman's frank self-assessment would no doubt be echoed by many reporters and pundits in the upper echelon of corporate media, if they too would respond honestly to public demands that they disclose "confidential sources" and other relationships with AIPAC. The mainstream corporate media's era of investigative journalism and honest Middle East reporting seems to have passed, and the "fourth estate" is no longer taking a businesslike approach to AIPAC. However, one member of the judiciary may possibly be hiking down the trail blazed by Fulbright.

Judge T.S. Ellis quashed the defense team's motion to dismiss based on the "rarity" of Espionage Act prosecutions. In their filing, the defendants claimed that there was no warning that Rosen and Weissman's or AIPAC's activities might be prosecuted since "past applications of the statute fail to provide fair warning that the statute could be applied to the facts alleged in the superseding indictment." [195] In other words, court dockets and news reports of other criminal prosecutions didn't signal to AIPAC that violations of U.S. criminal statutes in pursuit of their policy objectives would ever be punished.

Ellis made it clear that lack of prosecutions under any criminal statute is not a safe harbor or license for would-be criminals, including AIPAC officials:

> [T]hat the rarity of prosecution under the statutes does not indicate that the statutes were not to be enforced as written. We think in any event, the rarity of use of the statute as a basis for prosecution is at best a questionable basis for nullifying the clear language of the statute, and we think the revision of 1950 and its reenactment of section 793(d) demonstrate that Congress did not consider such statute meaningless or intend that the statute and its prohibitions were to be abandoned. [196]

This opinion is another major statement entirely missed by most observers of the trial, but one of hope for Americans wishing to see more investigations into and law enforcement action over "policy crimes." Judge Ellis may be signaling to the DOJ and grand juries across America that there should be a new willingness to prosecute criminal statutes AIPAC would rather see lying dormant, of which the two most relevant are the Logan Act and Foreign Agents Registration Act. No person or organization has ever been successfully prosecuted under the 1798 Logan Act, but the Logan Act clauses clearly prohibit core AIPAC lobbying activities it achieves only through coordinated communications and links to the Israeli government:

> Any citizen of the United States, wherever he may be, who, without authority of the United States, directly or indirectly commences or carries on any correspondence or intercourse with any foreign government or any officer or agent thereof, with intent to influence the measures or conduct of any foreign government or of any officer or agent thereof, in relation to any disputes or controversies with the United States, or to defeat the measures of the United States, shall be fined under this title or imprisoned not more than three years, or both.[197]

The Logan Act almost exactly describes AIPAC's daily behind-the-scenes activities in the US and overseas and prohibits them. It is impossible to know why no prosecutor has ever thought to indict AIPAC officials under Logan. Little investigation or discovery beyond reading evidence in the public domain would be necessary. Investigations of AIPAC since 1999 have probably already gathered enough wiretap, public domain, and other documentary evidence to indict the lobby for harmful "end runs" around U.S. policy in coordination with the Israeli government.

It could be troubling for AIPAC that the historical drought of Foreign Agents Registration Act indictments should no longer provide comfort. That FARA is an obscure and oft-abused law is not in doubt, especially after reading the transcript of the Fulbright investigation into why Jewish-Agency-funded US foreign agents did not register with the Justice Department or disclose their true financing, funding flows, and covert activities. FARA still defines foreign agents as follows:

> (1) any person who acts as an agent, representative, employee, or servant, or any person who acts in any other capacity at the order, request, or under the direction or control, of a foreign principal or of a person any of whose activities are directly or indirectly supervised, directed, controlled, financed, or subsidized in whole or in major part by a foreign principal, and who directly or through any other person—

(i) engages within the United States in political activities for or in the interests of such foreign principal;

(ii) acts within the United States as a public relations counsel, publicity agent, information-service employee or political consultant for or in the interests of such foreign principal;

(iii) within the United States solicits, collects, disburses, or dispenses contributions, loans, money, or other things of value for or in the interest of such foreign principal; or

(iv) within the United States represents the interests of such foreign principal before any agency or official of the Government of the United States; and

(2) any person who agrees, consents, assumes or purports to act as, or who is or holds himself out to be, whether or not pursuant to contractual relationship, an agent of a foreign principal as defined in clause (1) of this subsection.

In the 20 years leading up to 1992, only two rather insignificant FARA indictments lodged by the Department of Justice were widely publicized. The Department of Justice filed a third in 1992 against former Colorado legislator Sam Zakhem for promoting a "Stop Saddam" campaign with unreported Kuwaiti funds after Iraq's invasion of Kuwait in 1990.[198]

The public record documents numerous instances in which members of the Israel lobby received explicit instructions or acted as unregistered agents for various Israeli governments. The Middle East Peace Summit at Camp David took place between United States President Bill Clinton, Israeli Prime Minister Ehud Barak, and Palestinian Authority Chairman Yasser Arafat during the month of July in the year 2000. Ehud Barak's hurried calls to Israel lobby leaders in the U.S. to intervene whenever he felt pressured to make concessions during U.S. peace plan initiatives at Camp David are but one insignificant moment within a longstanding history of Israel lobby FARA violations. AIPAC's argument that they do not receive funding from overseas (or at least, not *anymore*) ring hollow. **"Agency" does not always require top-down payment flows from the principal to the foreign agent; only demonstrable policy direction and coordination are necessary to prove that AIPAC, like the American Zionist Council, is an unregistered foreign agent of the state of Israel.**

The American people, thought generally to ignore such esoteric issues, have expressed support for an AIPAC FARA registration in a statistically significant Zogby International poll conducted in the year 2004. In a Council for the National Interest (CNI) chartered poll, 61% of Americans "somewhat" to "strongly" agreed with the statement "AIPAC should be asked to register as an agent of a foreign government and lose its tax-exempt status." Eugene Bird, president of CNI, said of the survey:

> The poll shows serious doubts that Americans have about the activities of AIPAC. They strongly endorse the position that we have long held, that AIPAC should register as an agent of a foreign government and lose its tax-exempt status. For years, Congress has been duped by their illegal activities.[199]

However, since the day Judge T.S. Ellis threw down the gauntlet, no additional FARA or Logan Act indictments have been filed. The press, with few exceptions, has not clamored for more foreign-agent-related investigations. It may be overly optimistic to expect any. The mainstream media itself waded into the AIPAC espionage trial with novel disclosure demands that just about scuttled the prosecution's case.

Corporate Media Intervenes on AIPAC's Behalf

One of the reasons that the mainstream corporate media has not covered very much of the fascinating pre-trial maneuverings in the USA v. Rosen and Weissman case may be quite simple: as eager and unquestioning recipients of purloined information and "background material" allegedly passed by Rosen and Weissman, the mainstream corporate press is also on trial. Accordingly, behind the scenes and mainly out of sight, corporate media has intervened in the AIPAC espionage trial, though the Associated Press did report one major victory for itself and the defendants on April 17, 2007:

> Prosecutors suffered a setback yesterday in their case against two former pro-Israel lobbyists accused of violating the 1917 Espionage Act when a federal judge rejected the government's proposal for conducting much of the trial in secret. The presiding judge, T. S. Ellis III underscored the gravity of the situation: "If the prosecution decline[s] to submit any substitutions [for classified evidence] that you would ever make public, then maybe...I have to decide whether to dismiss the indictment, if that's the case."

Various elements of the Israel lobby trumpeted the ruling as a victory for free speech. However, it is useful to review not only the involvement of mainstream corporate media in trafficking classified information alleged in the

AIPAC espionage case, but also their past record and consistency regarding secret evidence in other high-profile criminal cases.

Mainstream media's formal legal foray into the AIPAC case was triggered by a government motion. On Feb. 16, 2007, federal prosecutors filed a Classified Intelligence Procedures Act (CIPA) motion with the contents sealed from public view. CIPA is an established process under which courts operate when classified information is expected to be used at trial. In response, defendants Rosen and Weissman filed a sealed motion to strike the CIPA requests and the government's motion to close the trial.

On March 13, 2007, attorney Jay Ward Brown filed a motion to intervene and argue against the Department of Justice prosecutors' proposal to "limit public access to classified portions of the trial proceedings." Brown filed the motion on behalf of elite media clients, including the Newspaper Guild, Communications Workers of America, the Radio-Television News Directors Association, Reuters America LLC, the Society of Professional Journalists, Time Inc., the *Washington Post*, the Hearst Corp., the Reporters Committee for Freedom of the Press, ABC, the American Society of Newspaper Editors, the Associated Press, Dow Jones & Company, and the Newspaper Association of America. The collective pressure and threat brought to bear on Judge Ellis was implicit in the motion: Any attempt to introduce classified evidence or protect sources and methods with closed proceedings would be widely reported on as Soviet-era secrecy in a kangaroo court.

Titled an "Emergency Motion for Leave to Intervene," the filing sought to keep the trial completely open, ostensibly in the public interest of press coverage (see Appendix #3). The motion also subtly expresses mainstream media preconceptions about the trial, stating in the filing that the case is worth coverage because of the "unusual factual circumstances that gave rise to their [Rosen and Weissman's] indictment" and that the case involves an "unprecedented application of the Espionage Act."[200]

Only on the surface can this seem to be a triumph of a free press over government secrecy: the involvement of key members of the elite media in the AIPAC espionage trial goes far beyond the intent of this motion or what they routinely report. A few of the same corporate news outlets filing the motion were willingly used by Weissman and Rosen to disseminate classified information to further AIPAC's policy objectives. On July 21, 2004, Weissman and Rosen called *Washington Post* reporter Glenn Kessler to pass information that they said was from "an American intelligence source" later revealed to be Col. Lawrence Franklin. Rosen relayed classified information to Reuters correspondent Carol Giacomo and *Washington Post* reporter Michael Dobbs about confidential drafts of a U.S. presidential directive advocating a more aggressive U.S. posture toward Iran. Dobbs included the classified information in a story two weeks later.

Another motion-to-intervene filer, the Reporters Committee for Freedom of the Press, clarified the mainstream corporate media's collective desire to continue serving as a willing and mostly blind conduit for selectively released, less than comprehensive classified information. According to Lucy

Dalglish, executive director of the Reporters Committee for Freedom of the Press:

> Journalists who cover national security and defense receive classified information all the time. It's virtually routine. If that were the standard for bringing an espionage case, we'd be locking up a lot of people in this town, and there would be fewer sources of information.[201]

Notwithstanding the press's apparent willingness to be used to further AIPAC's or any other lobby's policy objectives by selectively disclosing classified information, the media's objection to protecting classified information in an espionage trial raised consistency questions. Does the elite media's own reporting record reveal a consistent industry-wide commitment calling for disclosure of secret evidence in all high-profile criminal trials? It does not.

The *New York Times* in fact chided the Iran-Contra trial defense of Oliver North in an article titled "North's Lawyers Trying to Derail Prosecutor's Plan," published in 1989. Reporter Michael Wines reported:

> The federal judge in the Iran-contra case today rejected the bulk of Oliver L. North's demand to use 30,000 pages of secret documents as evidence in his defense, accusing Mr. North of making the request in a calculated effort to "frustrate the prosecution."[202]

Another motion filer, Time Inc., also had a different take on classified evidence in an earlier era. *Time* reporter George J. Church wrote in a piece called "Top-Secret Strategy" that the North defense appeal for public access to classified information was despicable "graymail." Church elaborated:

> North's strategy, it seems, is to threaten to disclose embarrassing secrets if the government will not drop the trial. In the bitter words of Robin Ross, chief aide to Attorney General Thornburgh, "This great American hero is graymailing the government. This is the guy who stood up in his Marine Corps uniform and all his medals, and now he is sticking it to the government with an advantage (knowledge of secrets) he got through service to his country."[203]

What about spies for foreign countries like Russia? According to the case docket of FBI spy for Russia Robert Hanssen, the mainstream corporate press did not at any time file urgent briefs, even though the bulk of the evidence trafficked by Hanssen to be used against him in court would have been highly classified.

In the tight-knit world of the elite corporate media, if a defendant like Oliver North who is not a "friend" or "confidential source" attempts to force the disclosure of classified information as evidence in his own defense, it is categorized as "graymail." When defendants Weissman and Rosen attempt to similarly force the revelation of classified information, possibly "outing" sources and methods used to protect the U.S. against Israeli espionage, media companies involved as "conduits" wade in with legal briefs calling for "freedom of the press." This double standard is unfortunate because of the actual public interests involved.

The stakes in the AIPAC espionage case could not be higher. If it finally goes to trial, reverberations could go far beyond AIPAC. The case could redefine the role of lobbies, the mainstream press, and think tanks operating in Washington, DC. It is not clear whether average Americans approve of Washington's hidden world of selective third-party disclosure and trafficking in classified information. When the question is raised, the public is mostly regaled with tales of selfless disclosure, such as Daniel Ellsberg's release of the Pentagon Papers discrediting the Department of Defense case for involving the military in Vietnam. Unfortunately, that and other patriotic acts do not remotely resemble the more routine political skullduggery involved in classified information leaks. It is known, but not widely appreciated, that selectively disclosed and leveraged classified information fed to the "free press" and reporters such as the *New York Times*' Judith Miller played a large role in promoting the Iraq invasion. Readers of mainstream press coverage about the Rosen and Weissman trial are not receiving enough information to ask whether there is a gaping difference between classified information leaks in the public interest and those solely in the interest of a foreign lobby. It is ironic that if the legal intervention of the corporate media had scuttled the Weissman and Rosen prosecution, the public would never have obtained answers to important questions concerning leaks. Lack of relevant reporting on AIPAC's activities ensures that the status quo of public oblivion and ignorance about how US Middle East policy is truly formulated continues.

Where Is the Espionage Case Headed?

Rosen and Weissman are presumed innocent until a judgment or decision states otherwise. One outcome is likely, however. Unlike the civil suit against AIPAC's election law violations regarding AstroTurf PACs, a criminal trial of this nature cannot simply languish in the legal system. It must either move to trial or be dismissed.

The judge in the case, T.S. Ellis, has maintained high hurdles for the prosecution team. Although the 1917 Espionage Act is broad, Ellis requires that the prosecution team prove that both "injury of the United States **and** the advantage of a foreign nation" occurred. The media and defense insistence that no CIPA proceedings be used in the trial has also led the prosecution to request declassification of evidence to be used in the trial. It is not currently known whether federal government agencies will cooperate with prosecution requests for declassification sufficiently to allow the trial to go forward.

The defense team also moved to have charges dismissed on Thompson Memorandum policy (guidelines for prosecuting corporations). Specifically, the defendants charged that AIPAC was encouraged to fire them and not apply its virtually unlimited resources, financial and human, to their defense under point four of the guidelines in force at the time of their indictment:

> 4. The corporation's timely, voluntary disclosure of wrongdoing and willingness to cooperate in the investigation of its agents, including waiver of corporate attorney client privilege and work product protection.[204]

In a May 2006 memorandum, Judge T.S. Ellis suggested that the Thompson guidelines assumed corporations advancing attorney fees would be seen as more culpable than organizations severing relationships with alleged wrongdoers.

> In short, the Thompson Memorandum suggests that an organization that advances attorneys' fees to an employee the government deems "culpable" is more likely to be prosecuted than a similarly situated organization that does not advance fees, unless the organization is required by law to advance fees.[205]

Weissman and Rosen offered via their defense team a written statement explaining that they felt their rights were violated, since the activities they routinely engaged in were, after all, part of AIPAC's mission. Somewhat like Lawrence Franklin, who might have taken the fall for Douglas Feith and Paul Wolfowitz, Rosen and Weissman signaled that they might have been set up to be punished and cut off as sacrificial lambs by AIPAC, which had been, after all, under investigation and threat of indictment as well. With AIPAC's history of avoiding brushes with the law and passing off illegal activity as "the work of junior staff," Rosen and Weissman clearly had good reason to believe AIPAC was still in favor of its old policy for escaping punishment: jettisoning or otherwise minimizing as "problem employees" operatives who were caught out on AIPAC missions gone awry. As summarized by Judge T.S. Ellis:

> During this period, the government was actively investigating defendants and AIPAC. Also during this period, defendants were employed by AIPAC—Rosen as

AIPAC's Director of Foreign Policy Issues, and Weissman as AIPAC's Senior Middle East Analyst. It was part of defendant's AIPAC duties to meet regularly with government officials of both the United States and Israel. Defendants contend that all of the conduct alleged in the indictment was within the scope of their employment with AIPAC and was undertaken with AIPAC's benefit.[206]

Rosen and Weissman retained legal counsel in 2004, as soon as the FBI began to interview them. The two have been billed monthly for legal fees ever since.[207] It is not known whether any of these fees have been deferred or discounted to lower rates pending the formation of a legal defense fund or anticipated renewal of AIPAC legal defense support. When the government's investigation became public knowledge, AIPAC promised to not only pay for, but to also advance Rosen and Weissman's attorneys' fees, as well as entering into a joint defense agreement signed on September 1, 2004.

AIPAC kept its payment promise only for "several months."[208] In the spring of 2005, AIPAC terminated Weissman and Rosen's employment and terminated the joint defense agreement, ceasing advances on attorneys' fees. This occurred, according to the defendants, because the prosecutors, following the Thompson memorandum then in force, intimated that AIPAC could be threatened with criminal charges or further intense scrutiny. In a "good cop, bad cop" style of negotiation, prosecutors allegedly offered to stop investigating AIPAC if it would cooperate with the government, including dropping legal fee support, compensation, and other assistance to the defendants. According to Judge T.S. Ellis:

> Specifically, defendants allege that in a December 2004 meeting with AIPAC officials, prosecutors stated that the investigation was analogous to one in the "corporate fraud arena," and they criticized AIPAC's leadership for "circling the wagons" by denying wrongdoing. Later, in a February 15, 2005 meeting, prosecutors allegedly stated that satisfactory cooperation with the prosecution would "get AIPAC out from under all this." Defendants allege these two statements confirm that AIPAC was at least a subject, if not a target, of the investigation. On March 18, 2005 defendants allege that then US Attorney Paul McNulty and an unnamed Assistant US Attorney told AIPAC counsel that AIPAC needed to fire the defendants. The next business day, March 21, 2005, AIPAC fired defendants and terminated the joint defense agreement, but intended to keep this fact secret from the public. Yet, AIPAC did inform the government of the terminations on March 22, 2005. In the words of AIPAC

counsel, this action was taken to gain "credibility with the government," i.e., to be able to claim compliance with the Thompson Memorandum.

On learning that defendants had been fired and the joint defense agreement terminated, prosecutors allegedly continued to inquire whether AIPAC was continuing to pay defendants' legal fees. At an April 29, 2005 meeting between AIPAC and the government to resolve the fees issue, defendants allege that the government pointedly asked AIPAC why it was paying defendants' legal fees, severance pay, and health benefits. According to defendants, AIPAC counsel responded that defendants could not otherwise afford counsel. Prosecutors allegedly indicated their displeasure on the fees matter and informed AIPAC counsel that it should not only cease paying defendants' attorneys' fees, but also cut off defendants' severance pay and benefits. Both AIPAC counsel and the prosecutors later confirmed to defense counsel that the government had raised the issue of AIPAC's payment of counsel fees and health benefits at the April 29 meeting. [209]

Weissman and Rosen claimed that this government pressure on AIPAC violated their constitutional rights: first, that it interfered with the defendants' Sixth Amendment right to expend resources toward a legal counsel of choice, and second, that they were deprived of due process of law, a violation of the Fifth Amendment.

In a long analysis, Judge Ellis referred to precedent and the fact that over almost two years of robust, novel, and exhaustive gambits for dismissal, the defendants appeared to have had adequate resources to retain and benefit from their counsel of choice. Paradoxically, prosecutor Paul McNulty, who so strictly applied the Thompson memorandum guidelines, subsequently changed the guidelines on January 12, 2006 after rising to become US Deputy Attorney General. Specifically, McNulty dropped the required show of "good faith" a corporation could achieve by ceasing support of allegedly bad-apple executives. Not even Judge Ellis would tackle the potentially sticky political aspects of whether McNulty was politically pressured to make the changes.

The McNulty Memorandum is more solicitous of organizational advances of attorneys' fees than its predecessor, stating that "prosecutors generally should not take into account whether a corporation is advancing attorney's fees to employees or agents under investigation or indictment," except in "extremely rare cases" where "the totality of the circumstances show that it was intended to impede a criminal investigation." P. McNulty, *Principles of Federal Prosecution of Business Organizations* (January 12, 2006), § VII ¶ B.3-B.3 n.3. **The practical, political, or other reasons that led the DOJ to change its policy on fee advances are not relevant to the constitutional analysis required here.**[210]

McNulty's looser set of guidelines for federal prosecution of business organizations no longer discourages corporations from supplying unlimited financial and legal resources for the defense of indicted executives except in extreme circumstances. From the perspective of AIPAC, McNulty's changes and Judge Ellis's opinion mean that AIPAC can now begin to apply its cash reserves and net assets (which in 2005 amounted to almost $50 million) and bring to bear a sympathetic army of brilliant legal minds and public relations experts arrayed across the country to win in the courtroom and the court of public opinion by any means necessary.

Still, McNulty's interactions with AIPAC raise many other questions. Why did US Attorney McNulty make deals with AIPAC that aligned so conveniently with its prior history of blaming major scandals and run-ins with the law on junior or rogue employees? Why didn't McNulty indict AIPAC if, as Rosen and Weissman asserted to Judge T. S. Ellis, their activities fell well within the scope of common practices at AIPAC? What would have happened if AIPAC were indicted?

In the past, in the corporate world, criminal indictment of a firm sometimes meant implosion, such as in the case of accounting firm Arthur Anderson. Chicago-based Arthur Anderson was once a "Big Five" accounting firm along with PricewaterhouseCoopers, Deloitte Touche Tohmatsu, Ernst & Young, and KPMG. Anderson's size and status meant it could easily gain and retain Fortune 500 business auditing accounts, preparing taxes and performing lucrative consulting services for large corporations. In 2002, the members of the firm had to voluntarily surrender their licenses to practice as Certified Public Accountants in the U.S. This occurred as collateral damage when Enron's massive fraud and accounting violations highlighted Anderson's fiduciary failures as an auditor. When the Department of Justice began prosecution of the energy giant, Anderson's days were numbered. **It is likely that such a criminal indictment of AIPAC would have brought about a similar implosion.**

However, the Department of Justice has developed an aversion to indicting large corporations, according to Russell Mokhiber of *Corporate Crime Reporter*. In his analysis, *20 Things You should Know About Corporate Crime*, based on two decades of information from the *Corporate Crime Reporter*, several principles appear to be operative in the treatment of AIPAC as an influential corporation:

> ..corporate crime lesson number one—prosecute corporate crime to achieve higher office, then prosecute

street crime to protect your political position. Or to simplify it, corporate crime is all about power politics.[211]

According to this principle, McNulty's indictment of two corporate criminals provided fuel for his own rise to higher levels in the DOJ. Rather than immediately focus on so-called "street crime," however, McNulty unwound the very tool that allowed him to indict Rosen and Weissman without having to bear the awesome wrath of AIPAC—the Thompson Memorandum. McNulty's later action gave the defendants a very good chance to "get out of jail free" and have the charges against them dropped. The defendants immediately saw this opening and attempted to exploit the change in guidelines. Whether it was an intentional bone thrown to the defendants or not, this fits the DOJ's general pattern of treading lightly with alleged corporate criminals. Mokhiber's second principle also appears to be operative in AIPAC's case:

> Corporate criminals are the only criminal class in the United States that have the power to define the laws under which they live.[212]

Drones and echoes of "implications for press and think tanks" noise are still reverberating in the press. Washington elite talking points about the antiquity of the 1917 Espionage Act are also floating around the edges of the courtroom. It is now within AIPAC's power to use its most powerful tool—influence over Congress—to modify the law so that it no longer restrains the activities of operatives such as Rosen and Weissman. To some extent, the law, or at least the section about prosecutorial discretion, has already been changed to favor the defendants. It did not require an act of Congress, and the McNulty Memorandum may have proven to be a get-out-of-jail-free card for an entirely different set of defendants—those indicted in a massive tax evasion case centered on another accounting firm, KPMG.

In early 2005, the United States Department of Justice accused KPMG LLP of fraud in marketing and establishing abusive tax shelters using offshore entities. Under a deferred prosecution agreement, KPMG LLP admitted to criminal wrongdoing in creating fraudulent tax shelters that helped wealthy clients, many sitting on oversize "Internet bubble" capital gains, avoid $2.5 billion in US taxes. KPMG agreed to pay $456 million in penalties in exchange for not having to face criminal prosecution. On January 3, 2007, the DOJ's criminal conspiracy charges against KPMG were dropped. Before the KPMG settlement, on the advice of its counsel, the firm found some "fall guys" to take the blame for activity within the corporate division set up to aggressively market the shelters. The parallels with AIPAC's strategy of ejecting Rosen and Weissman are uncanny. However, KPMG not only removed several tax partners, but also admitted unlawful conduct on behalf of the partners and agreed to cooperate with DOJ's investigation and help individually prosecute the former partners who had marketed and sold the tax shelters. KPMG went so far as to hire former US district judge Sven Erik Holmes to monitor its internal legal and regulatory affairs.

On June 25, 2007, the *Wall Street Journal* announced a scenario that might also soon occur in the AIPAC espionage case. The prosecutors simply gave up due to alleged Thompson Memorandum unfairness and appealed for leniency under the newly operative McNulty Memorandum guidelines.

> The KPMG tax-shelter case has taken another twist. Prosecutors have asked Judge Kaplan to dismiss indictments against a dozen former KPMG'ers on charges they sold illegal tax shelters. The move comes after Kaplan's ruling last year that the government violated the constitutional rights of the defendants during its investigation by pressuring KPMG to cut off their legal fees.
>
> "They're just giving up on everything," said David Spears, attorney for one of the KPMG defendants. "It's just stunning and very ungovernment-like."[213]

Rosen and Weissman could benefit from a similar legal reprieve or new Thompson-Memorandum-related initiatives launched with the new resources freed up by AIPAC. AIPAC can now intervene in Congress and finance the defense of its former employees without incurring DOJ wrath under the defunct Thompson Memorandum. AIPAC may be close to getting laws changed in its favor with the introduction of the Free Flow of Information Act of 2006.[214]

Legislation was sponsored by Senator Richard Lugar on May 18, 2006 to "guarantee the free flow of information to the public through a free and active press while protecting the right of the public to effective law enforcement and the fair administration of justice." It is possible that the defense team could try to portray Rosen and Weissman as individuals covered and by the Act which would protect:

> ...a person who, for financial gain or livelihood, is engaged in gathering, preparing, collecting, photographing, recording, writing, editing, reporting, or publishing news or information as a salaried employee of or independent contractor for a newspaper, news journal, news agency, book publisher, press association, wire service, radio or television station, network, magazine, Internet news service, or other professional medium or agency which has as one of its regular functions the processing and researching of news or information intended for dissemination to the public.[215]

Rosen and Weissman's information-gathering responsibilities, contributions to the *Near East Report*, and even authorship of content for the AIPAC website and media affiliates might be enough to shield their activities from scrutiny. The Act could prohibit compelled testimony against them from mainstream media recipients of purloined national defense information unless damage standards much higher than the Espionage Act could be proven, or it could be proven that "such unauthorized disclosure has seriously damaged the national security."[216] The Act seems to be uniquely tailored to AIPAC's claims that it pursues initiatives in the interest of the US and Israel, which it claims are "the same." It is also not surprising that the bipartisan group of lawmakers pushing this legislation collectively received over $1,330,774 in career Israel AstroTurf PAC money.[217]

This ability of all corporations under fire to benefit from subtle changes in the law and law enforcement and a pervasive resource imbalance is reflected in another Mokhiber corporate crime principle:

> Corporate crime is under-prosecuted by a factor of say—100. And the flip side of that—corporate crime prosecutors are under-funded by a factor of say—100.

AIPAC can now spend unlimited funds defending Rosen and Weissman and lobbying to have other US laws modified to make their prosecution moot. In AIPAC's worst-case scenario, if by some chance the defendants are convicted, other behind-the-scenes pressures brought to bear on the Bush administration could lead to a presidential pardon, or at very least, commutation. AIPAC can also deploy an army of lawyers and sympathetic top officials to lobby in an attempt to "slow roll" the declassification of evidence so that ultimately the prosecution and judge are frustrated and the charges are dismissed. The US attorneys prosecuting the case could also be convinced through internal politics at the Justice Department that it is simply not in the Bush administration's interest or that of an incoming Democratic president to precede with the prosecution. Whatever the outcome, at least a 100-to-1 resource imbalance favoring AIPAC has been unleashed by McNulty.

But again, what if Paul McNulty had originally suspected AIPAC was guilty of the crimes? According to Mokhiber's rules, this would simply not matter; powerful US corporations no longer really face the threat of indictment since Enron and Anderson fell. Far more common are deferred prosecution agreements and non-prosecution agreements:

> Corporations love deferred prosecution agreements. In the 1990s, if prosecutors had evidence of a crime, they would bring a criminal charge against the corporation and sometimes against the individual executives. And the company would end up pleading guilty. Then, about three years ago, the Justice Department said—hey, there is this thing called a deferred prosecution agreement. We can

bring a criminal charge against the company. And we will tell the company—if you are a good company and do not violate the law for the next two years, we will drop the charges. No harm, no foul. This is called a deferred prosecution agreement. And most major corporate crime prosecutions are brought this way now. The company pays a fine. The company is charged with a crime. But there is no conviction. And after two or three years, depending on the term of the agreement, the charges are dropped.

In pursuing AIPAC, McNulty had established a de facto deferred prosecution agreement under the guidelines of the now-defunct Thompson Memorandum. AIPAC dutifully jettisoned and cut off two of the most highly visible and convincing suspects as suggested by the Justice Department. Now that McNulty has undone the memorandum that kept AIPAC in check, even the appearance of a de facto non-prosecution agreement has evaporated along with any former verbal understandings. If history is any guide, it can be expected that massive behind-the-scenes pressure will be applied to terminate the case on AIPAC's terms. However, from AIPAC's perspective, it is more important than ever to suppress damaging information about its past while helping the defense team maneuver as quickly as possible for dismissal by any means.

Prosecutors and the bench are unlikely to ever hear any quantitative accounting of how AIPAC's illegal tactics harm America. In terms of damage, Mokhiber's rule #20 puts the true cost of private-sector corporate crimes in perspective:

Corporate crime inflicts far more damage on society than all street crime combined. Whether in bodies or injuries or dollars lost, corporate crime and violence wins by a landslide. The FBI estimates, for example, that burglary and robbery—street crimes—costs the nation $3.8 billion a year. The losses from a handful of major corporate frauds—Tyco, Adelphia, Worldcom, Enron—swamp the losses from all street robberies and burglaries combined. Health care fraud alone costs Americans $100 billion to $400 billion a year. The savings and loan fraud—which former Attorney General Dick Thornburgh called "the biggest white collar swindle in history"—cost us anywhere from $300 billion to $500 billion. And then you have your lesser frauds: auto repair fraud, $40 billion a year, securities fraud, $15 billion a year—and on down the list.

The cost of public-sector crime by actors such as AIPAC is less well known. The late Harvard economist Thomas Stauffer estimated the total cost of unnecessary and prolonged conflict in the Middle East at US $3 trillion. Stauffer lays a good deal of the blame for this at the doorstep of AIPAC:

> Conflicts in the Middle East have been very costly to the U.S., as well as to the rest of the world. An estimate of the total cost to the U.S. alone of instability and conflict in the region—which emanates from the core, Israeli-Palestinian conflict—amounts to close to $3 trillion, measured in 2002 dollars. This is an amount almost four times greater than the cost of the Vietnam war, also reckoned in 2002 dollars....
>
> Similarly, aid to Israel—and thus the regional total—also is understated, since much is outside of the foreign aid appropriation process or implicit in other programs. Support for Israel comes to $1.8 trillion, including special trade advantages, preferential contracts, or aid buried in other accounts. In addition to the financial outlay, U.S. aid to Israel costs some 275,000 American jobs each year...
>
> Another element is ad hoc support for Israel, which is not part of the formal foreign aid programs. No comprehensive compilation of U.S. support for Israel has been publicly released. Additional known items include loan guarantees—which the U.S. most probably will be forced to cover—special contracts for Israeli firms, legal and illegal transfers of marketable U.S. military technology, *de facto* exemption from U.S. trade protection provisions, and discounted sales or free transfers of "surplus" U.S. military equipment. An unquantifiable element is the trade and other aid given to Romania and Russia to facilitate Jewish migration to Israel; this has accumulated to many billions of dollars. Lastly, unofficial aid, in the form of transfers from the Diaspora resident in the U.S. and net purchases by U.S. parties of Israel Bonds, adds at least $40 billion to the total. A rough estimate, again a minimum, for such additional elements is more than $100 billion since 1973.
>
> U.S. jobs and exports also have been affected, adding to costs and losses. "Trade followed the flag" in the area—but in the reverse direction. As U.S. relations with Mideast countries deteriorated, trade was lost. Worsening

political relations resulted in the loss of hundreds of thousands of U.S. jobs. Some disappeared as a consequence of trade sanctions, some because large contracts were forfeited, thanks to the Israel lobby—as in the case of foregone sales of fighters to Saudi Arabia in the 1980s—and still others due to a dangerously growing trade-aid imbalance vis-à-vis Israel.[218]

The Ellis court has been reluctant to consider AIPAC's corporate history or outside expert damage assessments in the criminal trial. Two "friend of the court" or *amicus* briefs were offered in October of 2005 to outline larger public interests in the AIPAC espionage case: one on behalf of the defendants and an organization allegedly pushing "freedom of the press" concerns, and the other offered by the Institute for Research: Middle Eastern Policy, Inc. to reveal the historical context and consequences of AIPAC lawbreaking.

October 2005 Amicus Brief Order Summary
(Source USA v. Rosen and Weissman Order 2/27/2006)[219]

IN THE UNITED STATES DISTRICT COURT
FOR THE EASTERN DISTRICT OF VIRGINIA
Alexandria Division

UNITED STATES OF AMERICA,   )
)
                        v.   )   Case No. 1:05cr225
)
STEVEN J. ROSEN   )
KEITH WEISSMAN   )

ORDER

For its part, the Institute for Research has indicated that its *amicus curiae* brief, if permitted, would present the following points:

1. How AIPAC's organizational structure has evolved into a quasi intelligence service infiltrating the Executive Branch and Congress.

2. How AIPAC's operations on behalf of Israel make it an agent of foreign influence.

3. How AIPAC operations in the U.S. that promote ethnic cleansing of Palestinians and law-breaking overseas increase the potential of terrorist attacks against Americans.

See October 21, 2005 Letter from the Institute for Research, Re: Request to File Amicus Brief.

Judge Ellis ruled that neither organization had standing to file a full amicus brief without his authorization:

> Amicus briefs may also be helpful when the non party lacks a basis for intervention, but nonetheless possesses special information or a unique perspective not otherwise available to the court that would materially aid the court's decisional process....None of these circumstances exist here. Most importantly, the record reflects that the instant defendants are ably and energetically represented by counsel experienced in all facets of the case, including the constitutional challenge to § 793(e). The record also reflects that government counsel are similarly able, energetic and experienced.

None of these circumstances exist here. Most importantly, the record reflects that the defendants are ably and energetically represented by counsel experienced in all facets of the case, including the constitutional challenge to § 793(e). The record also reflects that government counsel are similarly able, energetic and experienced.

This is not to say that the two entities seeking amicus status do not have strong views about this prosecution or the statute's effect on their members' work. No doubt they do, as indeed it is likely that so, too, do many other interest groups, including other associations or committees of lawyers, law professors, journalists, lobbyists, editorial writers and many others. But the point is that this prosecution is not the appropriate procedural context in which various elements of society should debate the constitutional validity or wisdom of § 793(e). Nor is this prosecution an appropriate venue for non parties to advocate certain alleged facts they believe to be relevant to the case. While this is not the appropriate forum for the expression of interest group views, **there are ample appropriate *fora* for doing so, including the media in all its myriad forms, academia and, of course, the halls of Congress.**[vii] As the Seventh Circuit cogently put it, "Amicus briefs are often attempts to inject interest-group politics into the federal appellate process by flaunting the interest of a trade association or other interest group in the outcome of the appeal. *Scheidler*, 223 F.3d at 615."[220]

Judge Ellis ultimately denied permission for the filing of more detailed *amicus curiae*. His response demonstrated a failure to value the broader context and utility of a comprehensive and historically complete amicus filing entered into the formal court proceedings. AIPAC and its Israel lobby fellow travelers have so stymied debate on the core issues raised by the trial that a relevant hearing is no longer possible, either in the halls of Congress or in most of the mainstream news media. After receiving the amicus denial decision, IRmep urged the judge and prosecutors to consider the public interest stakes in the trial and not allow big media and political pressure to affect their willingness to continue the case. Judge T.S. Ellis then formally and specifically banned further "ex parte" communications to the court by the Institute for Research: Middle Eastern Policy, Inc. on April 23, 2007.

[vii] Author's emphasis.

However, in a gesture recognizing the importance of a critical analysis of the media's foray into the trial, the judge simultaneously insisted that both prosecutors and defense teams receive copies of the IRmep communication that triggered his order (see Appendix #4).

Six: Iraq Occupation and Iran

On the surface, AIPAC's visible lobbying activities seem little changed as the case against its two top officials grinds toward a trial date. AIPAC's 2007 policy conference was unaffected in terms of attendance by policymakers and high officials. Over 6,000 supporters attended, according to AIPAC. AIPAC also scored a major victory against opponents of a Bush administration preemptive war against Iran, as summarized by the *Washington Times*:

> Last week, House Speaker Nancy Pelosi received a smattering of boos when she bad-mouthed the war effort during a speech to the American Israel Public Affairs Committee, and the Democratic leadership, responding to concerns from pro-Israel lawmakers, was forced to strip from a military appropriations measure a provision meant to weaken President Bush's ability to respond to threats from Iran.[221]

Under the surface, it is also business as usual in Washington: criminal wrongdoing continues to corrupt America's core values, rule of law, and Middle East policy, as the Israel lobby's crosshairs shift almost completely toward Iran.

Fulbright's Hunch

Careful observers, with the benefit of nearly a half-century of hindsight, can see that Senator William Fulbright began to uncover something very big when he broadened his investigation from the Latin American and other country FARA questions originally publicized by Walter Pincus to include the operations, conduits, and movement of tax-exempt donations through the Jewish Agency. In 2005 former Israeli prosecutor Talia Sason released a wide-ranging study commissioned by the Israeli prime minister in which she documented a vast international money-laundering infrastructure centered within the Jewish Agency and controlled by the World Zionist Organization. These and other "charitable" organizations had laundered more than US $50 billion into illegal Israeli settlements while systematically expropriating and developing lands that did not belong to Israel. Reporting on the money-laundering scheme even reached *USA Today* in August of 2005:

JERUSALEM (AP)—Israel's effort since the 1967 Mideast war to fill the West Bank and Gaza Strip with Jews has grown from the scattered actions of zealous squatters into a network of 142 towns and villages that house nearly 240,000 people.

Now that Israel plans to spend some $2 billion to dismantle just 25 of the settlements—for which U.S. aid has been requested—it raises the question of how much money has been poured into populating these biblical lands with Jews, and exactly where it came from.

The official answer: No one knows.

Vice Premier Shimon Peres estimates Israel has spent about $50 billion since 1977, when the hard-line Likud government took over from his Labor party. Other former finance ministers and government officials don't discount a price tag—commonly floated but never documented— of $60 billion....

Despite its declared opposition to settlements, Washington only began taking action in the early 1990s, when Israel sought billions of dollars in U.S. loan guarantees. Washington said it would deduct sums that went into settlements dollar for dollar.

In 2003, when Israel was granted $9 billion in loan guarantees over three years, the cut was $289.5 million. Officials familiar with the issue, and speaking on condition of anonymity, say that low figure was reached with the help of the influential pro-Israel lobby, the American Israel Public Affairs Committee (AIPAC).

AIPAC officials refused to discuss the issue on the record, but denied they helped to negotiate the numbers.

Israel also used private U.S. donations for which it secured U.S. tax-exempt status, said David Newman, a political scientist at Israel's Ben Gurion University who researched settlement funding.

U.S. tax laws don't exempt donations for political activities such as settlements. Israel separated the World Zionist Organization from the quasi-governmental Jewish Agency, a move that allowed donors to inject money into settlements without losing tax exemptions. In reality, the two groups operate under one umbrella, with the same officials, departments and administrators overseeing the activities, Newman said.

Perhaps the grayest area is how Israel expropriated, confiscated or purchased land for settlements.[222]

The Jewish Agency's latest money-laundering scheme was designed to utilize US tax-exempt funds from donors to accomplish illegal ends overseas. The Sason report was not raised in the US Congress in 2005, thanks to the efforts of a foreign lobby the Jewish Agency funded back in the 1950s and 1960s. An earlier feeble attempt by the George H.W. Bush administration to punish Israel for illegal settlements in the 1990s was hobbled by AIPAC. Bush the elder's attempt is also thought to have partially contributed to his election loss and legacy as a one-term president. Only a few newspapers, such as *The Forward,* have fretted over the implications of the Sason report—specifically the lawbreaking by US charitable organizations tied to the World Zionist Organization and Jewish Agency:

Embarrassed leaders of American Jewish organizations were absorbing the news this week that an international body under their control was at the center of a tangled Israeli scheme, detailed in a bombshell government report, to build illegal settlement outposts in violation of Israeli law, policy and international commitments.

The international body, the World Zionist Organization, or WZO, is described in the report as a pivotal player in the scheme, in which midlevel officials in various government ministries secretly channeled funds and resources to the illegal West Bank outposts. Several sources told the Forward that a WZO department, the Settlement Division, was used as a vehicle for many of the illegal activities, in part because its status as a nongovernmental organization shielded it from government oversight....

WZO is a confederation of pro-Israel groups in dozens of countries, including such mainstays as Hadassah, B'nai B'rith and offshoots of the Reform and Conservative movements. American groups control 30% of the organization's main governing bodies, including the World Zionist Congress, which is convened in Jerusalem every four years.

> Most leaders of American Zionist groups said they had
> been unaware of the extent of WZO's work in the
> territories.[223]

The Forward need not have worried too much about the "embarrassed leaders" or subsequent investigations by US law enforcement. On November 21, 2005, top US law enforcement officials sent representatives to attend a comprehensive briefing organized by the Council for the National Interest in the Russell Senate Office about how US affiliates of charities such as B'nai B'rith and Hadassah were in direct control of the World Zionist Organization and directly linked to the massive money-laundering operation mentioned in the Talia Sason report. DOJ officials and Treasury officials were advised about the details of the money-laundering operation and how it was an indirect generator of terrorism against the United States as illegal settlements, low-intensity conflict, and hopelessness generated asymmetric retaliation against US interests.[224] Barry Sabin, chief of the US counterterrorism section, formally thanked the keynote speaker for the presentation and straightforward documentary evidence that could have led directly to indictments for money laundering and other violations of the US criminal code in 2005 (see Appendix #5). **To date, however, US law enforcement officials have visibly done nothing to slow or prosecute the parties responsible for this new (and yet very old) charitable money-laundering operation. Two of the officials assigned to attend the briefing have been transferred, one to the Anti-Trust division.** [225] This follows an established pattern of law enforcement failures present since the Fulbright foreign agent hearings.

There was a brief moment in 1963 when strict enforcement of FARA could have terminated foreign financing and regulated the Israel lobby in the United States. However, Cold War priorities captivated the attention of Congress, and the institution Steven Rosen would refer to as a "night flower"[226] spread its tendrils with little public scrutiny. Fulbright became a target of this foreign lobby after his extraordinary investigation, but he was not its only victim in the Senate. William Stuart Symington served as the first Secretary of the Air Force from 1947 until 1950 and was a Democratic United States Senator from Missouri from 1953 until 1976. Non-enforcement in the face of obvious violations undermined Symington's centerpiece nuclear arms control legislation.

The Symington Amendment was adopted in 1976. This amendment to Sec. 101 of the Arms Export Control Act[227] was intended to fortify and extend the Nuclear Non-Proliferation Treaty. The act prohibited most US assistance to any country found trafficking in nuclear enrichment equipment or technology outside of international safeguards. Israel never signed the Nuclear Non-Proliferation Treaty, since it would be an admission that it possessed nuclear weapons. Although the Symington Amendment was intended to put the brakes on countries such as Pakistan, if honestly applied, the Symington Amendment would also prohibit US aid to Israel unless waived and exempted by the US president. Instead, the US, which knows about Israel's clandestine nuclear weapons development, stockpile, and launch capabilities but chooses not to publicly acknowledge these weapons, following Israel's own policy of "strategic ambiguity." By ignoring US laws such as the Symington Amendment, Congress is further undermining its reputation as a legislative body concerned with the rule of law. AIPAC is instrumental in maintaining this subterfuge.

Ignoring or selectively applying laws such as the Symington Amendment, US criminal law, and UN Security Council resolutions also diminishes the US in the international arena. The US has a long record of undermining UN general assembly attempts to address matters related to Israel's adherence to international law, particularly violations of UN resolutions and human rights. The US's disregard for the rule of law also highlights double standards and hampers US policies that are unrelated to Israel. This AIPAC-powered policy has torn down the United States and exposed the hypocrisy of many US initiatives across the globe, but most particularly in the Middle East. Going against the current of US and international law could not have been accomplished without intent and financial resources.

The money laundering present at the birth of AIPAC continues, but the flow has reversed course. Instead of laundering foreign funds into the US, American nonprofit groups, including many evangelical Christian nonprofits, launder funds overseas, effectively waging a secret war of expropriation and ethnic cleansing against Palestinians. They count on lobbying pressure by AIPAC for protection of these operations, no matter how much damage they cause to the US. WINEP devotes special attention to producing and flooding the news media with "flak"[228] about money laundering. However, the core of the problem, according to WINEP, is not the $50 billion laundered to create chaos in Palestine—it is Iranian money laundering.

WINEP's special team for keeping a focus on Iran and money laundering are Michael Jacobson and Stuart A. Levey. According to his byline in a recent article published in the *Jerusalem Post* titled "What to Do about Teheran's Money-Laundering," Jacobson actively consults with the Treasury Department to formulate US tactics:

> The writer is a senior fellow in the Stein program in terrorism, intelligence and policy at The Washington Institute for Near East Policy and a former senior advisor in Treasury's Office of Terrorism and Financial Intelligence.[229]

WINEP strongly backed the nomination of Stuart Levey to the newly created position of "Under Secretary of the Treasury for Terrorism and Financial Intelligence." Levey was confirmed by the Senate on July 21, 2004. Levey frequently travels to Israel[230] to work on international money-laundering issues, but not by sitting down with Talia Sason or tackling sticky issues of US tax-exempt laundering. On his most recent trip, Levey kept a tight focus on Iran, with laudatory support from WINEP:

> Stuart Levey, the US Treasury official spearheading efforts to hit Iran economically, met with Foreign Minister Tzipi Livni in Tel Aviv on Thursday to discuss the ongoing efforts to get the world's financial institutions to sever ties with Teheran.
>
> Israeli officials said Levey's work, which is conducted outside of the UN framework, was important because it could be pursued without facing obstacles placed in the way by Russia and China, whose support is necessary for UN sanctions. They agreed with US assessments that China is the most reluctant UN Security Council member when it comes to supporting expanded sanctions against Iran's nuclear program.
>
> Levey, the US undersecretary of the treasury for terrorism and financial intelligence, has spent the last couple of years trying to convince major financial institutions in the US and around the world to employ financial sanctions against Teheran.[231]

The revelations of the Sason report reveal clearly that US nonprofits indirectly controlling the Jewish Agency violate US criminal statutes forbidding "expeditions against a friendly nation." US criminal code clearly prohibits such activity:

> Whoever, within the United States, knowingly begins or sets on foot or provides or prepares a means for or furnishes the money for, or takes part in, any military or naval expedition or enterprise to be carried on from thence against the territory or dominion of any foreign prince or state, or of any colony, district, or people with whom the United States is at peace, shall be fined under this title or imprisoned not more than three years, or both.[232]

The low-intensity warfare against Palestinians financed by US tax-exempt organizations and promoted by AIPAC occurs only because of the United States' complete unwillingness to enforce its own laws. AIPAC's "consultants" such as Michael Jacobson and the disingenuousness of officials like Stuart Levey in key positions make a difference. Americans are left wondering how many armchair generals are marching in Israel and AIPAC's policy Foreign Legion. A recent confidential report from a departing UN official highlights the danger of entering battle as skirmishes begun by AIPAC's shock troops conflate into regional war.

Conclusion: A United Nations Exit Report

US law enforcement officials have squandered numerous opportunities to regulate AIPAC in the public interest. When Fulbright uncovered money laundering of tax-exempt funds into the US for foreign propaganda and lobbying, the FARA violations were documented well enough for grand jury consideration and indictments. Instead, a series of well-documented violations were placed into the record and nothing more useful was done. This allowed a sense of impunity to develop in the US Israel lobby that continues to this day. It also allowed foreign guidance and "start-up" money channeled through byzantine conduits to establish the iron superstructure of a foreign interest lobby. This lobby has used complex corporate structures, secret coordination, and foreign-directed lobbying to anticipate and block US initiatives to resolve burning Middle East issues while channeling unwarranted foreign aid to Israel. The foreign-directed campaign against the Johnson plan uncovered by the Fulbright investigation should have served as an early warning of further damage on the horizon if the illegal activities of the lobby went unchecked. **Instead, 40 years on, the lobby acts with even more brazen impunity while Palestinian refugees enter their second, third, and fourth generations living in the squalor and hopelessness of refugee camps.**

There are now few US State Department officials who would dare commit to paper the real reasons for stunning reversals and blockades of US policy by the Israel lobby. The lobby's power has grown to the point that AIPAC related officials such as Dennis Ross and Martin Indyk and fellow travelers such as Douglas Feith and Paul Wolfowitz formulate and execute US policy on behalf of the lobby. However, clarity about the corrosive influence of the Israel lobby on the US and Middle East nevertheless emerges from other quarters from time to time.

A confidential copy of a 52-page "End of Mission Report" filed by United Nations Special Coordinator for the Middle East Peace Process Alvaro de Soto in May of 2006 is unequivocal about how the Israel lobby's officials in the United States have hampered any advancements by the so-called "Quartet." The United States, Russia, the EU, and the UN have been unable to achieve any benchmarks elaborated in their "Roadmap for Peace":[233]

There is a curious, asymmetric coincidence between Israel and the Palestinians regarding the US's third-party role in negotiations between them: when push comes to shove Israel can accept an intrusive US third-party role because they know that the US is a close ally which can be counted on not to betray it or even pull any surprises—

the US usually floats proposals with the Israelis before presenting them to the Palestinians. Israelis also take advantage of their unique ability to influence the formulation of US policy...[234]

The fact is that even-handedness has been pummeled into submission in an unprecedented way since the beginning of 2007.

De Soto blamed the US and Israel lobby appointees for putting negative pressure on the UN, including crude threats to financing, unless the UN agreed to special treatment for Israel and economic embargo of any legally elected Palestinian government if it included Hamas.

The Envoys met at 10 AM on 30 January in preparation for the Principals' meeting in the evening. I was subjected to a heavy barrage from Welch and Abrams, including ominous innuendo to the effect that if the Secretary-General didn't encourage a review of projects of UN agencies and programmes it could have repercussions when UN budget deliberations took place on Capitol Hill.

In negotiating with Elliot Abrams, a Bush administration National Security Advisor, de Soto was, in effect, negotiating with a member of a long-term family dynasty of the Israel lobby. Married to Rachel Decter, the daughter of neoconservative maven Midge Decter, the spouse of *Commentary* magazine founder Norman Podhoretz, Abrams is the last of a line of extremist neoconservative advisors brought into the Bush administration who are still exercising power. Abrams appeared among several signers of a letter to President Clinton in 1998 urging military action against Iraq on the pretext of "weapons of mass destruction"[235]. Abram's mother-in-law Midge Decter's first husband, Moshe Decter, was investigated by Fulbright for receiving $12,000 yearly from the Jewish Agency and $5,000 from the Israeli Consulate.[236] Moshe Decter also served for a time as the editor of the *Near East Report*.[237] In a letter subpoenaed by Fulbright and entered into the Senate record, Moshe Decter sternly instructed the Jewish Agency on how to properly structure his unregistered conduit payments through the American Jewish Congress:

As you undoubtedly know, my annual fee is $12,000 which is paid to me through the mechanism of the American Jewish Congress. Since the Congress is good enough to do this service to me and the Agency, it is only proper that they should be accommodated as to the mode of payment which they prefer.[238]

Eliot Abrams, now married into the Decter clan, has had his own brushes with the law. Abrams was convicted of two misdemeanor counts for lying to the American Congress about the Iran-Contra affair while he served in the Reagan administration. Abrams's policy guidance backed major human rights violations and atrocities in Central America in the 1980s that led to a complex US-Israel-Iran scheme to provide Nicaraguan militants with arms now curiously referred to as only the "Iran-Contra" scandal. His ideology was fundamental in conceptualizing and implementing the human chaos touched off by the US invasion of Iraq.

The appointment of Abrams was an obscure process contingent on behind-the-scenes lobbying that elevated him based on his Israel lobby bona fides. Public display of these credentials are found in his 1997 book *Faith or Fear: How Jews can Survive in a Christian America,* which he wrote while working at the Hudson Institute from 1991-1996. This fretful diatribe against assimilation reveals the internal struggle of a militarist eager to involve others in his highly personal religious war for self-identity. Abrams refers to Israel throughout the book as a driving force of that identity.

> If this is not, in itself, a form of anti-Semitism, it nevertheless explains a great deal about the lack of sympathy many American Jews feel toward American Christianity. For millions of Jews, Israel is a tremendously emotional matter, and in many cases a source of their Jewish identity. It is very difficult to credit as sympathetic to Jews and Judaism those who are totally unsympathetic to Israel. This is not a matter of theology.[239]

Abrams excoriates critics of Israeli policy. He also takes to task the Anti-Defamation League's 1994 attack on Christian conservatives as a tactical blunder,[240] emphasizing the importance of alliances with Christian evangelicals in spite of their belief that in the End Times Jews must convert to Christianity or disappear in the Rapture.

> ...evangelicals are strongly pro-Israel. In fact, after American Jews, the strongest supporters of Israel in the United States are white evangelical Protestants. Roughly a quarter of them visit Israel every year, meaning that most American visitors to Israel are Christians, not Jewish. Yet the support of most Jews for Israel is based, even if indirectly, on their religious affiliation; why can Christians not, with equal legitimacy, have the same motivation? Many Jews argue that evangelicals favor Jewish control of the Holy Land because they see it as a step toward the messianic era when Jesus returns, and therefore as a means to an end inimical to Judaism. But

the support itself is surely no less valuable or authentic. Even those (indeed, perhaps especially those) who do not expect the return of Jesus promised in the New Testament must see that Christian support for Israel is founded in a belief that guarantees continuing dedication to Israel's well-being.[241]

Abrams's definition of the model life in America and self-identity is strongly coupled with ties to Israel and keeping the gates of funding wide open.

A model Jew in America is not off in the synagogue at prayer but out at a meeting discussing a new hospital, a trip to Israel, or a new fund-raising drive.[242]

Support for Israel became central to Jewish identity—"the core of the religion of American Jews." To many American Jews, it became the essence of their lives as Jews and of their understanding of their own Jewishness. They loved Israel, and they supported Israel. A good Jew could do no less, and one who did no less—and no more—was a good Jew.[243]

Part of Abrams's core ideology is that the absence of the threat of military calamity diminishes the "cement" that holds Israel together. He remembers the founding of the state in 1948 and the 1967 Six-Day War as important moments of conflict-induced bonding and worries that the absence of perceived or real threats will diminish identity.

Yet many question whether that cement will prove to be permanent, and in fact there is evidence that it is already losing strength. First, the American Jewish sentiment about Israel grew as the risks to Israel grew, reaching its highest and most intense levels as a result of the 1967 and 1973 wars. It is in that sense a commitment to the survival of Israel-in-danger; it is more properly denominated pro-Israelism than Zionism. As it today far exceeds the level of support that Israel enjoyed prior to 1948 or from 1948 to 1967, perhaps it exceeds the level Israel will enjoy in the future if American Jews conclude that Middle East peace efforts have greatly diminished the threat to its security. In that event, the intensity of concern about Israel-in-danger, and its centrality to the Jewishness of many American Jews, may well fade.[244]

For Abrams, absence of war for survival is not the only problem. The absence of anti-Semitism, a term he does not define in order to use it as a broad but flexible truncheon, is also paradoxically a huge problem according to his book.

> Thus, a deep-seated fear of Christianity and an expectation of anti-Semitism remain central to the "Jewishness" of many American Jews. For them, Jewishness does not consist of belief in traditional Judaism; instead, at the core it means not being Christian. That negative identity is strengthened by fearful presumptions about Christian attitudes toward Jews and their place in American society.
>
> The problem with anti-Semitism as a source of Jewish identity is that with a decrease of prejudice those shored-up ramparts will collapse—and this is precisely what is happening in the United States...Those days are over and they will not return.[245]

The Bush administration has largely followed the twisted policy prescriptions of Abrams: studiously avoiding any serious Middle East peace process, constantly and hysterically highlighting even the most fanciful threats to Israel while creating a real one by invading Iraq, and harnessing the political power of the evangelical Christian multitudes. Abrams's recent policy work has been tightly focused on advancing the case for a US attack on Iran from within the offices of the George W. Bush administration. De Soto summarized how the work of ideologues like Abrams and the Bush administration's tight focus on advancing counterintuitive Israel-centric policy objectives created a benchmark for evaluating UN performance that has been actively marketed and repeated by major think tanks and policy pundits:

> "At almost every juncture a premium is put on good relations with the US and improving the UN's relationship with Israel. I have no problem with either goal but I do have a problem with self-delusion," he writes. "Forgetting our ability to influence the Palestinian scene in the hope that it keeps open doors to Israel is to trade our Ace for a Joker."

Elliot Abrams and other prominent neoconservatives are in positions of power because of AIPAC support and opaque lobbying. Congress and the executive branch have largely stopped opposing Israel lobby candidates for key positions, with some notable exceptions such as John Bolton's proposed nomination as UN ambassador. Within the UN, the US is seen as pushing the common objectives of ideologues like Bolton rather than formulating policy in the interest of all Americans. Former insider James Baker commented to de Soto on the negative environment this creates in international peace negotiations:

> A few months after I began my assignment, at the commemoration of the tenth anniversary of the Rabin assassination, I bumped into James Baker, whom I had dealt with on El Salvador and Western Sahara. I asked him whether he had any advice for me. He said only, "Be strong. These guys can small weakness a mile away." Sound advice, even if you represent the UN rather than the superpower. What he was warning against, clearly, was the tendency that exists among US policy makers and even amongst the sturdiest of politicians to cower before any hint of Israeli displeasure, and to pander shamelessly before Israeli-linked audiences.[246]

Just as de Soto's private lament echoes State Department protests over the Israel lobby's burial of the Johnson plan in the early 1960s, Rosen and Weissman's dismissal gambits cover ground that was already covered in that earlier era. When confronted with incontrovertible evidence of wrongdoing by Fulbright's foreign agent investigation, AIPAC, the Jewish Agency, and the American Zionist Council bobbed and weaved and laid down excuses. Hadn't the complex intertwined corporate archipelago created in 1960 made Israel lobby FARA violations legal? When faced with blatant, documented contradictions, an old standby was also put into service: "I don't recall."[247] Rosen and Weissman's challenges to the 1917 Espionage Act are remarkably similar to the defense presented by the Jewish Agency's legal council in the Fulbright hearing. Maurice M. Boukstein revealed his contempt for the law to Senator Fulbright when he proposed that the Foreign Agents Registration Act itself was flawed and inapplicable to the intertwined corporate entities he had designed:

Senator Fulbright: Mr. Boukstein, you haven't enlightened me as to how we may deal with this matter because you only confirmed my view that under the existing law and practices, at least, as they are illustrated here, it completely thwarts the purpose of the Foreign Agents Registration Act, because we are not given any information—neither the public or government—as to the nature of these activities and the nature of these projects for which this registrant here is supplied the money.

Mr. Boukstein: Mr. Chairman, if you would go back to the time when the Foreign Agents Act was made law, in 1938, I think the purpose was altogether different. The language, of course, comprehends everybody; but the purpose at the time was to bring out, into the open, subversive, at that time particularly Nazi activities, and I hope that the law in this respect served its purpose.

But to the extent that it is still law and to the extent that it is to be applied to other purpose, I certainly agree with you that it needs considerable modification and change.[248]

In fewer words, "the law is deeply flawed, and even if it weren't, these organizations and their members are above it." And so goes the core justification for a multitude of violations that make America and the world a more dangerous and unjust place. No matter that many Americans and people across the world now hear the Israel lobby's drumbeat for US military action in Iraq, Iran, and Syria. Even as America's foreign aid and electoral principles are violated; US law is simply not applied to the Israel lobby. To even notice or mention the lobby now often brings retaliatory charges of anti-Semitism. To criticize the lobby is to be held up as the moral equivalent of a Nazi. Lamentably, ample warning has been given that this sad day would eventually arrive.

The US Senate observes George Washington's birthday by reading aloud the founding father's 7,641-word Farewell Address in legislative session. In his final 1796 letter, informally addressed to "Friends and Citizens" of the United States Washington warned that the forces of geographical sectionalism, political factionalism, and interference by foreign powers in the nation's domestic affairs could threaten the stability and viability of the republic. He urged Americans to exercise diligence in subordinating such forces to the common national interest.

> So likewise, a passionate attachment of one nation for another produces a variety of evils. Sympathy for the favorite nation, facilitating the illusion of an imaginary common interest in cases where no real common interest exists, and infusing into one the enmities of the other, betrays the former into a participation in the quarrels and wars of the latter, without adequate inducement or justification. It leads also to concessions to the favorite nation of privileges denied to others, which is apt doubly to injure the nation making the concessions, by unnecessarily parting with what ought to have been retained, and by exciting jealousy, ill-will, and a disposition to retaliate, in the parties from whom equal privileges are withheld. And it gives to ambitious, corrupted, or deluged citizens (who devote themselves to the favorite nation), facility to betray or sacrifice the interests of their own country, without odium, sometimes even with popularity; gilding with the appearances of a virtuous sense of obligation, a commendable deference for public opinion, or a laudable zeal for public good, the

base or foolish compliances of ambition, corruption, or infatuation.[249]

The dire international situation in the Middle East is a direct result of America's consistent failure to enforce laws that were established for very sound reasons: to limit and regulate the power of foreign interests over the legislative and executive branches. George Washington's firm admonition has been read aloud in the US Senate every year since 1896, but is neither heard nor comprehended. No nation that so selectively enforces its own laws to favor a powerful elite—in this case, an illegal lobby founded by, funded by, and in the service of a foreign state—can long maintain the confidence and cooperation of the governed. Forty years after the findings of the Fulbright investigation, it is time to put an end to this illegal foreign lobby that has long flouted US law and suborned the national interest as a foreign agent.

Appendix

#1 1963 Fulbright Hearings Report Cover

ACTIVITIES OF NONDIPLOMATIC REPRESENTATIVES OF FOREIGN PRINCIPALS IN THE UNITED STATES

HEARINGS

BEFORE THE

COMMITTEE ON FOREIGN RELATIONS
UNITED STATES SENATE

EIGHTY-EIGHTH CONGRESS

FIRST SESSION

UNDER THE AUTHORITY OF S. RES. 362, 87TH CONGRESS,
AND S. RES. 25, 88TH CONGRESS, AUTHORIZING THE COM-
MITTEE ON FOREIGN RELATIONS TO STUDY THE ACTIV-
ITIES OF NONDIPLOMATIC REPRESENTATIVES OF
FOREIGN PRINCIPALS IN THE UNITED STATES

Part 1

MARCH 13 AND JUNE 20, 1963

Printed for the use of the Committee on Foreign Relations

COMMITTEE ON FOREIGN RELATIONS

J. W. FULBRIGHT, Arkansas, *Chairman*

JOHN SPARKMAN, Alabama	BOURKE B. HICKENLOOPER, Iowa
HUBERT H. HUMPHREY, Minnesota	GEORGE D. AIKEN, Vermont
MIKE MANSFIELD, Montana	FRANK CARLSON, Kansas
WAYNE MORSE, Oregon	JOHN J. WILLIAMS, Delaware
RUSSELL B. LONG, Louisiana	KARL E. MUNDT, South Dakota
ALBERT GORE, Tennessee	
FRANK J. LAUSCHE, Ohio	
FRANK CHURCH, Idaho	
STUART SYMINGTON, Missouri	
THOMAS J. DODD, Connecticut	
GEORGE A. SMATHERS, Florida	

CARL MARCY, *Chief of Staff*
DARRELL ST. CLAIRE, *Clerk*

Note.—This hearing was held in executive session, and released
August 1, 1963, pursuant to committee determination.

#2 AIPAC Lebanon War Fundraising

From the Desk of **Howard Friedman** | AIPAC President

July 30, 2006

Look what you've done!

My Fellow American,

As I'm writing to you, Israel is fighting a pivotal war for her life.

It's a battle imposed on her by terrorist organizations that seem to have adopted their disregard for human life (including the lives of their own people) from tales of the barbaric tribes of old.

The expected chorus of international condemnation of Israel's actions came almost on cue:

Yes, Europe conceded that Israel may actually be right this time — BUT:

> Israel's reaction to more than 100 rockets falling *daily* on its major cities is decidedly "disproportionate." "There must be a cease-fire immediately!" they cried.

> > Only ONE nation on earth came out immediately and said:
> > "Israel has *every* right to defend itself!"

> > Only ONE nation on earth came out and flatly declared:
> > **Let Israel finish the job. A premature cease-fire will only allow Hizballah to re-arm once more, leading to future attacks.**

That nation is the United States of America — and the reason it had such a clear, unambiguous view of the situation is <u>YOU and the rest of American Jewry.</u>

<u>Make no mistake about it!</u>

A strong and secure Israel is vital to America's interests. And American Jews use their democratic right to communicate that message to their elected officials. The organization which fosters that communication is AIPAC, America's pro-Israel lobby. Through AIPAC, Americans have the opportunity to voice their support and lobby for America's ONLY <u>true</u> ally in the Middle East.

<u>How do we do it?</u>

of long, hard work which never ends. U.S. support of Israel isn't automatic:

- Acting on behalf of Americans like you, AIPAC hosts educational events on Capitol Hill, offering information and analysis on Middle East issues and the Israeli-Palestinian conflict to members of Congress and their staffs.

- "Seeing is believing." AIPAC's educational foundation sponsors trips to Israel for elected officials, political pundits, influential columnists, candidates for office and political advisors.

  If they are going to make decisions regarding Israel or write about her — let them see what really is taking place on the ground!

- Members of Congress, staffers and administration officials have come to rely on AIPAC's memos. They are VERY busy people and they know they can count on AIPAC for clear-eyed analysis of the issues that pertain to the U.S.-Israel relationship.

  And so, we purchase newspapers, magazines, and books...we attend seminars and workshops...all to gain a *comprehensive* understanding of ALL the issues affecting the U.S.-Israel relationship. We then present this information in concise form to elected officials. The information and analysis are impeccable — after all, our reputation is at stake. This results in policy and legislation that make up Israel's lifeline.

- AIPAC meets with every candidate running for Congress. These candidates receive in-depth briefings to help them completely understand the complexities of Israel's predicament and that of the Middle East as a whole.

  We even ask each candidate to author a "position paper" on their views of the U.S.-Israel relationship — so it's clear where they stand on the subject!

- And to ensure the future, AIPAC's award-winning student program gives our nation's future decision-makers and activists the information, training and skills they need to be effective pro-Israel advocates.

  You saw the results with the immediate response of the United States — as opposed to the rest of the world, where our brethren don't have "an AIPAC."

Unfortunately, our work has just begun!

Back in 1948, Golda Meir said that Israel's secret weapon in its war with the Arabs was one simple fact — "We have nowhere else to go."

Let's face it, Israel **must** win this war <u>decisively</u>. It has no other choice. A cease-fire — without the disarming of Hizballah — would be a failure. It would allow the terrorists to re-group, re-arm and resume their attacks.

Don't forget, it was Hizballah that blew up 241 American troops in Lebanon in

Next page please...

1983 — and they haven't stopped killing since. They've taken over southern Lebanon, tearing it away from the Lebanese people and holding them hostage.

They have built an arsenal of more than 12,000 rockets — which they shoot at Israeli cities at an average rate of over 100 a day! They have hit Haifa, Israel's 3rd largest city — and they have the long-range rockets (and the desire) to hit Tel Aviv as well. **Millions of Israelis are in Hizballah's sights.**

Hizballah must be defeated.

Unfortunately, we have very little time left to act:

- The international community is already starting to apply pressure on Israel to sign a cease-fire agreement prematurely.

- United Nations officials are going so far as to accuse Israel of purposefully targeting U.N. peacekeepers in Lebanon — an outlandish accusation... even by U.N. standards.

- It's only a matter of time before the anti-Israel rhetoric begins spreading across college campuses, peppering the college press and conversations across the campus commons.

There is only one organization uniquely positioned to deal with these formidable challenges. That organization is AIPAC, **but we are only as strong as your support.**

But even these aren't the hardest — or most urgent — tasks facing us!

The war is a diversion!!!

Yes, the war is real enough — just ask the people of northern Israel who live in their bomb shelters day and night.

Yes, the war is real — just take a look inside the hospitals in Israel, filled with a growing list of casualties.

Yes, the war is real and yes, it must be won emphatically and immediately...

But ultimately, the war is acting as a distraction!!!

You see, Hizballah is Iran's proxy. It was created and has been trained and funded by Iran from its beginnings to today.

Iran undoubtedly rejoices that Hizballah started a war with Israel because:

This war is a convenient way to divert attention and international pressure away from Iran's nuclear weapons program!

Iran has supplied Hizballah with its current arsenal. This includes everything from sophisticated radar-guided missiles to mid-range rockets capable of striking Tel Aviv... *Just imagine what the current conflict would look like if Iran had the ability to provide Hizballah with a nuclear weapon.*

- Now is the time for us, American Jews, to stand up and tell our elected officials that they must demand Iran halt its pursuit of atomic arms.

- Now is the time to make sure that support for Israel's war effort doesn't wane.

- Our work has yielded marvelous support for Israel — as you can see — yet, our work has just begun. This is why I'm writing you this letter today.

This is a call to action: Israel needs us now more than ever!

AIPAC's efforts require significant resources. But we, the Jews of America, have no choice. This is why we need your support right now.

You have an important opportunity to influence U.S.-Israel relations through AIPAC — Use it!

Do it...because it's your democratic right as a proud American.

Do it...because it's our sacred duty as American Jews.

Israel needs us now. Every day the pressure mounts on our representatives to give in. We can't let it happen!

Please join AIPAC today by making the most generous investment you can possibly afford. Yes, **investment**. It's an investment in Israel's future...an investment in your rights as a proud American Jew...and an investment in world peace and security for us and our children.

I'm waiting anxiously for your positive and most generous response.

Sincerely Yours,

Howard Friedman
AIPAC President

#3 Corporate Media's Legal Intervention into USA v. Rosen and Weissman

IN THE UNITED STATES DISTRICT COURT
EASTERN DISTRICT OF VIRGINIA
Alexandria Division

UNITED STATES OF AMERICA	
vs.	No. 1:05-cr-225 (TSE)
STEVEN J. ROSEN, KEITH WEISSMAN,	
Defendants.	
REPORTERS COMMITTEE FOR FREEDOM OF THE PRESS; ABC, INC.; AMERICAN SOCIETY OF NEWSPAPER EDITORS; THE ASSOCIATED PRESS; DOW JONES & COMPANY, INC.; NEWSPAPER ASSOCIATION OF AMERICA; THE NEWSPAPER GUILD, COMMUNICATIONS WORKERS OF AMERICA; RADIO-TELEVISION NEWS DIRECTORS ASSOCIATION; REUTERS AMERICA LLC; SOCIETY OF PROFESSIONAL JOURNALISTS; TIME INC.; AND THE WASHINGTON POST,	
Movant-Intervenors.	

EMERGENCY MOTION FOR LEAVE TO INTERVENE WITH RESPECT TO PROPOSED CLOSURES OF TRIAL PROCEEDINGS AND RECORD

Come now as Movant-Intervenors the Reporters Committee for Freedom of the Press; ABC, Inc.; the American Society of Newspaper Editors; the Associated Press; Dow Jones & Company, Inc.; the Newspaper Association of America; the Newspaper Guild, Communications Workers of America; the Radio-Television News Directors Association; Reuters America LLC; the Society of Professional Journalists; Time Inc.; and The Washington Post and, for their

motion for leave to intervene in this criminal proceeding for the limited purpose of being heard in connection with the government's apparent request to close the trial, and any other pending or future motion seeking to restrict public and press access to the trial proceedings or the record thereof, respectfully state:

1.   This is a criminal prosecution under the Espionage Act of two individuals, former lobbyists for the American Israel Public Affairs Committee ("AIPAC"), who allegedly conspired to transmit information relating to the national defense to individuals not authorized to receive it, under circumstances where there was reason to believe the information could be used to the injury of the United States or to the advantage of a foreign nation. Trial in this action is set to commence on June 4, 2007. There is intense public interest in these proceedings, in part because of the defendants' association with AIPAC and the unusual factual circumstances that gave rise to their indictment, and because the case involves an unprecedented application of the Espionage Act that may test the reach of the statute as a tool to prosecute recipients of national security leaks who subsequently disclose to others what they have learned.

2.   Each of the Movant-Intervenors has an interest in these proceedings that arises out of the news coverage provided by their employees and/or members regarding this case in particular and national-security prosecutions more generally. Those employees and members expect to provide the public with regular news reports regarding this prosecution through their respective broadcasting, print and Internet properties.

3.   On December 14, 2006, the Court issued a modified scheduling order that set a Classified Information Procedures Act ("CIPA") hearing for 11:00 a.m. on March 15, 2007. (Dkt. # 392.) On February 16, 2007, the government filed a "Motion for Hearing Pursuant to CIPA Section 6," the contents of which are sealed from public view. (Dkt. # 426.) Apparently in response to that motion, on Friday, March 9, 2007, defendants filed an "Under Seal and In Camera Motion to Strike the Government's CIPA 6(c) Requests and to Strike the Government's Request to Close the Trial," which likewise is unavailable to members of the public. (Dkt. # 442.) Defendants' motion -- docketed by the Clerk on Monday, March 12, 2007 -- provided the first notice to non-parties that there was a request before the Court to restrict public access to the trial. Later on March 12, the Court entered an order that granted defendants' motion to suspend the CIPA schedule pending resolution of defendants' motion opposing the government's proposed trial procedures and specified that the March 15 hearing would address defendants' challenge to the government's proposed trial procedures. (Dkt. # 443.) That order did not indicate whether the hearing would be open to members of the press and the public.

4.   Prior to Monday, March 12, 2007, there was no indication on the public docket that this hearing would address matters beyond the scope of CIPA.

5.   Intervention is the appropriate vehicle for the news media and other members of the public to vindicate their constitutionally protected access rights in the context of criminal proceedings. A news organization moving to intervene in these circumstances must be afforded a prompt and full hearing on such a motion. Denying intervention and a meaningful opportunity for the press and the public to be heard would render any closure of the proceedings

5.   Intervention is the appropriate vehicle for the news media and other members of the public to vindicate their constitutionally protected access rights in the context of criminal proceedings. A news organization moving to intervene in these circumstances must be afforded a prompt and full hearing on such a motion. Denying intervention and a meaningful opportunity for the press and the public to be heard would render any closure of the proceedings constitutionally invalid.

WHEREFORE, and for the reasons more fully set forth in the accompanying memorandum of points and authorities, the Movant-Intervenors respectfully request that the Court consider and grant their motion to intervene on an expedited basis and make such accommodations to the schedule in this action as are necessary to afford the Movant-Intervenors a reasonable opportunity to review the substance of the government's request and the

defendants' opposition thereto (and any other pending or future motion seeking to restrict public and press access to the trial proceedings or the record thereof) and to provide briefing and argument to the Court on the closure and/or sealing issues presented therein.

Dated: March 13, 2007

Respectfully submitted,

LEVINE SULLIVAN KOCH & SCHULZ, L.L.P.

By: _____
Jay Ward Brown, Va. Bar No. 34355
Ashley I. Kissinger
John B. O'Keefe, Va. Bar No. 71326
1050 Seventeenth Street, NW, Suite 800
Washington, DC 20036
Telephone: (202) 508-1100
Facsimile: (202) 861-9888

Counsel for Movant-Intervenors

#4 Response to IRmep's Ex Parte Filing on Media Influence in USA v. Rosen and Weissman

**IN THE UNITED STATES DISTRICT COURT
FOR THE EASTERN DISTRICT OF VIRGINIA**
Alexandria Division

MAY – 2 2007

U.S. DISTRICT COURT
ALEXANDRIA, VIRGINIA

UNITED STATES OF AMERICA,	)	
	)	
v.	)	**Case No. 1:05cr225**
	)	
STEVEN J. ROSEN, and	)	
KEITH WEISSMAN,	)	
Defendants.	)	
	)	

ORDER

The Court has received a *ex parte* letter and article from the Institute for Research: Middle Eastern Policy commenting on the CIPA proceedings in this matter and on the related motions to intervene. Such *ex parte* communications are inappropriate and will not be read by the Court, and indeed, will hereafter be returned to the sender.

For good cause,

It is hereby **ORDERED** that the Clerk is **DIRECTED** to send a copy of the *ex parte* letter and article to all counsel of record.

The Clerk is further **DIRECTED** to return to the sender any subsequent *ex parte* submissions received from the Institute for Research: Middle Eastern Policy.

The Clerk is further **DIRECTED** to send a copy of this Order to all counsel of record and to the Institute for Research: Middle Eastern Policy.

May 2, 2007
Alexandria, Virginia

T. S. Ellis, III
United States District Judge

#5 Gratitude Without Action: The DOJ Counterterrorism Chief

U.S. Department of Justice

Criminal Division

Counterterrorism Section   *Washington, D.C. 20530*

December 7, 2005

Mr. Grant F. Smith
Director of Research
Institute for Research: Middle Eastern Policy
Calvert Station, PO Box 32041
Washington, DC 20007

Dear Mr. Smith:

Thank you for your letter of October 4, 2005. Attorney General Gonzales forwarded your letter, as well as the attached research notes, to the Criminal Division's Counterterrorism Section for a response.

We appreciate your hard work in researching links between money laundering and Middle Eastern violence as well as the implications on the security of the United States. As you know, the Department of Justice is very involved in efforts to ensure that tax exempt entities are not involved in funding violence or engaging in other non-charitable functions.

Two members of my staff recently attended a briefing given by the Institute for Research: Middle Eastern Policy at which you spoke on these issues and obtained a copy of the distributed materials. I also understand that an attorney from the Counterterrorism Section has recently been in touch with you regarding your work. Please do not hesitate to contact us if you have any additional questions or concerns.

Thank you again for bringing this matter to our attention.

Sincerely,

Barry M. Sabin, Chief
Counterterrorism Section

Index

Sources

[1] Internal AIPAC memo, cited in the Jerusalem Post, 24 August, 2004.

[2] William J. Fulbright, The Arrogance of Power, page 96, 1967

[3] US Code TITLE 18, PART I, CHAPTER 37, § 794 Gathering or delivering defense information to aid foreign government http://assembler.law.cornell.edu/uscode/html/uscode18/usc_sec_18_00000794----000-.html

[4] The SourceWatch and public-consensus-developed Wikipedia definition of "Astroturf" and "Astroturfing" is that these are terms for formal public relations campaigns in politics and advertising that seek to create the impression of spontaneous grassroots behavior. The reference to AstroTurf (artificial grass) is a metaphor to indicate fake grassroots support.

The goal of such a campaign is to disguise the agenda of a client as an independent public reaction to some political entity—a politician, political group, product, service, or event. Astroturfers attempt to orchestrate the actions of apparently diverse and geographically distributed individuals, by both overt ("outreach," "awareness," etc.) and covert (disinformation) means. Astroturfing may be undertaken by anything from an individual pushing a personal agenda to highly organized professional groups with financial backing from large corporations, nonprofits, or activist organizations.

[5] John Mearsheimer and Stephen Walt, The Israel Lobby and U.S. Foreign Policy, Kennedy School of Government, Harvard University, 2006

[6] Ellis, Judge T.S., Memorandum Opinion, USA v Steven J. Rosen AND Keith Weissman, 8 May, 2007

[7] William J. Lanouette, The National Journal, May 13, 1978

[8] US Department of Justice Foreign Agent Registration Unit Public Office registration number 208

[9] US Department of Justice Foreign Agent Registration Unit Public Office registration number 543 Recent FARA filings of other foreign agents reveal that the Israeli Consulate was formerly listed as "Israel Information Service." See page 122 of the 2003 FARA office report to Congress: http://www.usdoj.gov/criminal/fara/reports/December31-2003.pdf

[10] I.L. Kenen, letter to Senator William Fulbright, Senate Foreign Relations Committee investigation into the Activities of Agents of Foreign Principals in the United States, page 1779, letter dated September 6, 1963

[11] Senate Foreign Relations Committee investigation into the Activities of Agents of Foreign Principals in the United States, pages 1350, May 23, 1963

[12] I.L. Kenen, letter to Senator William Fulbright, Senate Foreign Relations Committee investigation into the Activities of Agents of Foreign Principals in the United States, page 1779, letter dated September 6, 1963

[13] Senate Foreign Relations Committee investigation into the Activities of Agents of Foreign Principals in the United States, pages 1235, May 23, 1963

[14] Steven Spiegel, pp. 87-9. The Other Arab-Israeli Conflict

[15] Reuters/Chicago Tribune, March 25, 1988

[16] David Glenn, Columbia Journalism Review, March/April 2006

[17] Walter Pincus email to the author, August 9, 2007.

[18] Walter Pincus email to the author, August 9, 2007.

[19] Lawrence Mosher, National Observer (Dow Jones), May 19, 1970

[20] Senate Foreign Relations Committee investigation into the Activities of Agents of Foreign Principals in the United States, pages 1228, May 23, 1963

[21] Senate Foreign Relations Committee investigation into the Activities of Agents of Foreign Principals in the United States, pages 1216-1217, May 23, 1963

[22] Senate Foreign Relations Committee investigation into the Activities of Agents of Foreign Principals in the United States, page 1320, May 23, 1963

[23] Senate Foreign Relations Committee investigation into the Activities of Agents of Foreign Principals in the United States, pages 1307-1312, May 23, 1963

[24] Zakai Shalom, Pages 31-32, Ben-Gurion's Political Struggles, 1963-1967 a Lion in Winter

[25] Page 123, Joan Comay, Lavinia Cohn-Sherbok, Who's Who in Jewish History

[26] Senate Foreign Relations Committee investigation into the Activities of Agents of Foreign Principals in the United States, page 1735, August 1, 1963

[27] Senate Foreign Relations Committee investigation into the Activities of Agents of Foreign Principals in the United States, page 1735, August 1, 1963

[28] Senate Foreign Relations Committee investigation into the Activities of Agents of Foreign Principals in the United States, page 1735, August 1, 1963

[29] Senate Foreign Relations Committee investigation into the Activities of Agents of Foreign Principals in the United States, page 1211, May 23, 1963

[30] Senate Foreign Relations Committee investigation into the Activities of Agents of Foreign Principals in the United States, page 1258, May 23, 1963

[31] I.L. Kenen, letter to Senator William Fulbright, Senate Foreign Relations Committee investigation into the Activities of Agents of Foreign Principals in the United States, page 1737-1738

[32] Senate Foreign Relations Committee investigation into the Activities of Agents of Foreign Principals in the United States, pages 1735-1741, August 1, 1963

[33] IRS Form 990, Near East Research, Inc, Fiscal year ending September 30, 2005

[34] Senate Foreign Relations Committee investigation into the Activities of Agents of Foreign Principals in the United States, page 1326-1328, May 23, 1963

[35] Senate Foreign Relations Committee investigation into the Activities of Agents of Foreign Principals in the United States, page 1343, May 23, 1963

[36] Senate Foreign Relations Committee investigation into the Activities of Agents of Foreign Principals in the United States, page 1344, May 23, 1963

[37] Senate Foreign Relations Committee investigation into the Activities of Agents of Foreign Principals in the United States, page 1344, May 23, 1963

[38] Senate Foreign Relations Committee investigation into the Activities of Agents of Foreign Principals in the United States, page 1344, May 23, 1963

[39] Senate Foreign Relations Committee investigation into the Activities of Agents of Foreign Principals in the United States, page 1346, May 23, 1963

[40] Senate Foreign Relations Committee investigation into the Activities of Agents of Foreign Principals in the United States, page 1347, May 23, 1963

[41] Senate Foreign Relations Committee investigation into the Activities of Agents of Foreign Principals in the United States, page 1347, May 23, 1963

[42] Senate Foreign Relations Committee investigation into the Activities of Agents of Foreign Principals in the United States, page 1347, May 23, 1963

[43] Senate Foreign Relations Committee investigation into the Activities of Agents of Foreign Principals in the United States, page 1344, May 23, 1963

[44] Senate Foreign Relations Committee investigation into the Activities of Agents of Foreign Principals in the United States, page 1345, May 23, 1963

[45] Senate Foreign Relations Committee investigation into the Activities of Agents of Foreign Principals in the United States, page 1345, May 23, 1963

[46] In 1940, Robert Soblen and his brother Jack were sent to America via Canada by Soviet Secret Police Chief Lavrenty Beria. During World War II, Robert Soblen provided the Soviets with secret documents from the Office of Strategic Services and data from the Sandia nuclear weapons development center at Albuquerque, New Mexico. In December 1960, the FBI arrested him on a charge of wartime espionage, which could have carried a death sentence, but did not consider him to be a flight risk. Soblen fled to Israel in June 1962, touching off a national debate in Israel over whether it should extradite any criminals for prosecution unless they could be returned to serve time in Israel.

[47] Senate Foreign Relations Committee investigation into the Activities of Agents of Foreign Principals in the United States, page 1345, May 23, 1963

[48] Senate Foreign Relations Committee investigation into the Activities of Agents of Foreign Principals in the United States, page 1355, May 23, 1963

[49] Senate Foreign Relations Committee investigation into the Activities of Agents of Foreign Principals in the United States, page 1346, May 23, 1963

[50] Senate Foreign Relations Committee investigation into the Activities of Agents of Foreign Principals in the United States, page 1346, May 23, 1963

[51] Senate Foreign Relations Committee investigation into the Activities of Agents of Foreign Principals in the United States, pages 1347-1348, May 23, 1963

[52] Senate Foreign Relations Committee investigation into the Activities of Agents of Foreign Principals in the United States, pages 1348-1350, May 23, 1963

[53] Senate Foreign Relations Committee investigation into the Activities of Agents of Foreign Principals in the United States, pages 1695-1696, August 1, 1963

[54] Senate Foreign Relations Committee investigation into the Activities of Agents of Foreign Principals in the United States, page 1701, August 1, 1963

[55] Yearbook of the United Nations, Office of Public Information, United Nations, New York, 1961

[56] Memorandum from the Assistant Secretary of State for Near Eastern and South Asian Affairs (Talbot) to Secretary of State Rusk/1/Washington, September 20, 1962. /1/Source: Department of State, Central Files, 325.84/9-2062. Secret. Drafted by Strong and cleared by Cleveland.

[57] Senate Foreign Relations Committee investigation into the Activities of Agents of Foreign Principals in the United States, pages 1704-1705, August 1, 1963

[58] Senate Foreign Relations Committee investigation into the Activities of Agents of Foreign Principals in the United States, page 1705, August 1, 1963

[59] Senate Foreign Relations Committee investigation into the Activities of Agents of Foreign Principals in the United States, pages 1704-1709, August 1, 1963

[60] Lucy Komisar, Pacific News Service, October 4, 2001

[61] Senate Foreign Relations Committee investigation into the Activities of Agents of Foreign Principals in the United States, page 1281, May 23, 1963

[62] Senate Foreign Relations Committee investigation into the Activities of Agents of Foreign Principals in the United States, page 1219, May 23, 1963

[63] Senate Foreign Relations Committee investigation into the Activities of Agents of Foreign Principals in the United States, page 1343, May 23, 1963

[64] Senate Foreign Relations Committee investigation into the Activities of Agents of Foreign Principals in the United States, page 1320, May 23, 1963

[65] Senate Foreign Relations Committee investigation into the Activities of Agents of Foreign Principals in the United States, pages 1709-1710, August 1, 1963

[66] The Senate record consistently refers to the "Council on Middle **Eastern** Affairs" and "**Sch**wadran" (as opposed to Shwadran).

[67] Senate Foreign Relations Committee investigation into the Activities of Agents of Foreign Principals in the United States, pages 1711-1713, August 1, 1963

[68] Senate Foreign Relations Committee investigation into the Activities of Agents of Foreign Principals in the United States, pages 1709-1710, August 1, 1963

[69] Senate Foreign Relations Committee investigation into the Activities of Agents of Foreign Principals in the United States, page 1262, May 23, 1963

[70] Dr. Khidhir Hamza, Director, Council on Middle Eastern Affairs, testimony before the House Armed Services Committee, United States House of Representatives, September 29, 2002

[71] No form 990 tax return exists in the central online repository GuideStar.org to indicate a corporate entity called the Council on Middle Eastern Affairs actually existed in the year 2002.

[72] Senate Foreign Relations Committee investigation into the Activities of Agents of Foreign Principals in the United States, pages 1367-1368, May 23, 1963

[73] Senate Foreign Relations Committee investigation into the Activities of Agents of Foreign Principals in the United States, page 1286, May 23, 1963

[74] Senate Foreign Relations Committee investigation into the Activities of Agents of Foreign Principals in the United States, pages 1287-1288, May 23, 1963

[75] Senate Foreign Relations Committee investigation into the Activities of Agents of Foreign Principals in the United States, pages 1741-1755, August 1, 1963

[76] Senate Foreign Relations Committee investigation into the Activities of Agents of Foreign Principals in the United States, pages 1742, August 1, 1963

[77] Senate Foreign Relations Committee investigation into the Activities of Agents of Foreign Principals in the United States, page 1228, May 23, 1963

[78] Senate Foreign Relations Committee investigation into the Activities of Agents of Foreign Principals in the United States, page 1235, May 23, 1963

[79] William J. Fulbright, The Arrogance of Power, page 4, 1967

[80] William J. Fulbright, The Arrogance of Power, page 96, 1967

[81] Lawrence Mosher, National Observer (Dow Jones), May 19, 1970

[82] Washington Report on Middle East Affairs, February 2, 1998

[83] Mitchell Bard, "Israeli Lobby Power," Midstream, Vol. 33, No. 1 (January 1, 1987)

[84] http://www.cptech.org/ip/health/phrma/301-00/israel.html

[85] Walt Mearsheimer, The London Review of Books, March 23, 2006

[86] Lawrence Mosher, National Observer (Dow Jones), May 19, 1970

[87] Stuart Auerbach, The Washington Post, August 3, 1984

[88] Stuart Auerbach, The Washington Post, August 3, 1984

[89] Michael J. Sniffen, The Associated Press, August 3, 1984

[90] Mark Hosenball, Footwear Industry News, October 1, 1984

[91] Michael J. Sniffen, The Associated Press, August 3, 1984

[92] Mark Hosenball, Footwear Industry News, October 1, 1984

[93] Robert J. Kaiser, May 27, 1984

[94] Deseret News, March 20, 2001

[95] Businessweek, May 7, 2001

[96] IRNA, October 25, 2001

[97] Charles R. Babcock, Washington Post, November 14, 1988

[98] Douglas Frantz and James O'Shea, Chicago Tribune, November 18, 1986

[99] Steve Neal, Chicago Sun-Times, February 16, 1992

[100] Douglas Frantz and James O'Shea, Chicago Tribune, November 18, 1986

[101] Kenneth Reich, Los Angeles Times, December 15, 1988

[102] Charles R. Babcock, Washington Post, November 14, 1988

[103] Kenneth Reich, Los Angeles Times, December 15, 1988

[104] Kenneth Reich, Los Angeles Times, December 15, 1988

[105] Kenneth Reich, Los Angeles Times, December 15, 1988

[106] GOLAND V. UNITED STATES; UNITED STATES V. GOLAND, Federal Elections Commission http://www.fec.gov/law/litigation_CCA_G.shtml

[107] Kenneth Reich, Los Angeles Times, 15 December 1988.

[108] GOLAND V. UNITED STATES; UNITED STATES V. GOLAND, Federal Elections Commission http://www.fec.gov/law/litigation_CCA_G.shtml

[109] GOLAND V. UNITED STATES; UNITED STATES V. GOLAND, Federal Elections Commission http://www.fec.gov/law/litigation_CCA_G.shtml

[110] Kenneth Reich, Los Angeles Times, December 15, 1988

[111] Kenneth Reich, Los Angeles Times, December 15, 1988

[112] Robert Pear with Richard L. Berke, New York Times, July 7, 1987

[113] Robert Pear with Richard L. Berke, New York Times, July 7, 1987

[114] Robert Pear with Richard L. Berke, New York Times, July 7, 1987

[115] Charles R. Babcock, Washington Post, November 14, 1988

[116] Charles R. Babcock, Washington Post, November 14, 1988

[117] Charles R. Babcock, Washington Post, November 14, 1988

[118] Facts on File World News Digest, December 2, 1988

[119] Charles R. Babcock, Washington Post, November 14, 1988

[120] Charles R. Babcock, Washington Post, November 14, 1988

[121] Fred Kaplan, Boston Globe, November 2, 1988

[122] Wall Street Journal, January 13, 1989

[123] Facts on File, Sunday Oregonian, February 17, 1989

[124] Associated Press, January 12, 1989

[125] St. Louis Post-Dispatch, January 15, 1989

[126] Washington Report on Middle East Affairs, January/February 1997

[127] Wolf Blitzer, January 13, 1989, Jerusalem Post

[128] Press Conference, Federal News Service, January 12, 1989

[129] Lucille Barnes, Washington Report on Near East Affairs, February 1991

[130] Larry Cohler, Washington Jewish Week, December 28, 1990

[131] Lucille Barnes, Washington Report on Near East Affairs, February 1991

[132] Richard Curtiss, Washington Report on Near East Affairs, January/February 1997

[133] Richard Curtiss, Washington Report on Near East Affairs, January/February 1997

[134] Federal News Service, August 12, 1992

[135] Federal News Service, August 12, 1992

[136] Seth Gitell, Forward, June 5, 1998

[137] Judge T.S. Ellis, III, US vs. Steven J. Rosen and Keith Weissman, Memorandum Opinion, August 9, 2006

[138] PR Newswire, July 30, 2007

[139] TITLE 26 > Subtitle A > CHAPTER 1 > Subchapter F > PART I > § 501 § 501. Exemption from tax on corporations, certain trusts, etc. http://www.law.cornell.edu/uscode/html/uscode26/usc_sec_26_00000501----000-.html

[140] TITLE 26 > Subtitle A > CHAPTER 1 > Subchapter F > PART I > § 501 § 501. Exemption from tax on corporations, certain trusts, etc. http://www.law.cornell.edu/uscode/html/uscode26/usc_sec_26_00000501----000-.html

[141] Voice of America, 12/29/2006, http://www.irmep.org/voa8.htm

[142] 9/11 Commission Report

[143] Walt, Mearsheimer, The London Review of Books, March 23, 2006

[144] Miami Herald, 8/28/1999

[145] Michael Massing, The Nation, June 10, 2002

[146] Peter Stone, The National Journal, August 31, 1993

[147] Fortune Magazine, December 1997

[148] LA Times, May 8, 1998

[149] Michael Massing, The Nation, June 10, 2002

[150] Senate Foreign Relations Committee investigation into the Activities of Agents of Foreign Principals in the United States, page 1275, August 1, 1963

[151] Jim Abourezek, The Christian Science Monitor, January 26, 2007

[152] Power Trips Database, Center for Public Integrity, http://www.publicintegrity.org/powertrips/default.aspx?act=faq

[153] I.L. Kenen, letter to Senator William Fulbright, Senate Foreign Relations Committee investigation into the Activities of Agents of Foreign Principals in the United States, page 1779-1780, letter dated September 6, 1963

[154] I.L. Kenen, letter to Senator William Fulbright, Senate Foreign Relations Committee investigation into the Activities of Agents of Foreign Principals in the United States, page 1779-1780, letter dated September 6, 1963

[155] A search for "Near East Report" references in books can be made searching http://books.google.com/books?q=%22Near+East+Report%22&lr=&sa=N&start=40

[156] Elena Gontar, cponline.com, August 28, 2006

[157] Real Estate Weekly, December 7, 2005
[158] Mark Milstein, Washington Report on Middle East Affairs, July 1991
[159] Mark Milstein, Washington Report on Middle East Affairs, July 1991
[160] http://www.irmep.org/hispanic.htm#_edn5
[161] Andrew Ross Sorkin, New York Times, September 5, 2004
[162] Phyllis Berman, Forbes Magazine, December 8, 2006
[163] AIPAC Board Members on WINEP's Board as listed in 2004 IRS form 990
filings include Robert Asher, Paul Baker, Edward Levy, Mayer Mitchell, Larry
Mizel, Lester Pollack, Nina Rosenwald, Eugene Schupak, Roseelyne Swig, James
Tisch, Larry Weinberg, Tim Wurlinger and Harriet Zimmerman
[164] Joel Beinin, Le Monde Diplomatique, July 2003
[165] Ross, Dennis, Baltimore Sun, March 19, 2003
[166] Brian Whitaker, The Guardian, August 19, 2002
[167] For an early glimpse of Wolf Blitzer in his advocacy role, see the video
http://www.youtube.com/watch?v=2-8aTGnjHnI
[168] Forbes Magazine, September 21, 2006
[169] Director's Introductory Video, Brookings Saban Center Website,
http://www.brook.edu/fp/saban/overview.htm
[170] Brookings Institution form 990 filing for its fiscal year ending June 30, 2005
[171] Brookings Saban Center Website, http://www.brook.edu/fp/saban/overview.htm
[172] Profile of Pollack from the WINEP website archived at
http://web.archive.org/web/19980203173918/www.washingtoninstitute.org/senior/
pollack.htm
[173] Martin Indyk, Los Angeles Times, December 19, 2002
[174] Media Matters, July 30, 2007
[175] University of Albany community website
http://greatdanesforisrael.wordpress.com/2007/06/22/summer-aipac-saban/
[176] Susan Schmidt and Robin Wright, Washington Post, September 2, 2004
[177] Justin Raimondo, September 3, 2004
[178] Eric Lichtblau, The New York Times, October 6 2005
[179] Bradley Graham and Thomas E. Ricks, The Toronto Star, August 28, 2004
[180] Larisa Alexandrona, Raw Story, January 30, 2006
[181] Juan Cole, Informed Comment, August 29, 2004
[182] Julian Borger, The Guardian, July 17, 2003
[183] The New York Sun, August 2, 2007
[184] Walter Pincus, Washington Post, April 11, 2006
[185] Walter Pincus email to the author, August 9, 2007.
[186] US vs. Steven J. Rosen and Keith Weissman, Reporter's Transcript, Motions
Hearing, March 24, 2006
[187] Judge T.S. Ellis, III, US vs. Steven J. Rosen and Keith Weissman, Memorandum
Opinion, August 9, 2006
[188] The RAND Corporation (a contraction of the words "Research and
Development") is a think tank set up by the US Air Force in 1946 to perform
analysis and research for the United States military.
[189] Judge T.S. Ellis, III, US vs. Steven J. Rosen and Keith Weissman,
Memorandum Opinion, August 9, 2006

[190] Judge T.S. Ellis, III, US vs. Steven J. Rosen and Keith Weissman, Memorandum Opinion, August 9, 2006

[191] Judge T.S. Ellis, III, US vs. Steven J. Rosen and Keith Weissman, Memorandum Opinion, August 9, 2006

[192] Corrections, Washington Post, April 29, 2006

[193] The Institute for Research: Middle Eastern Policy demanded a correction from Walter Pincus over his misquote of US criminal statute in an article about the US v. Rosen and Weissman trial that was published on March 24, 2006. When Pincus refused, IRmep initiated a demand for correction with the Washington Post's Ombudsman, which eventually appeared in the Washington Post on April 29, 2006, more than a month after the error first appeared. Since the ombudsman process is a public exercise in preserving journalistic integrity on behalf of readers, we present the email chain in reverse chronological order.
****

From: "Deborah C Howell"
To: Grant Smith
Sent: Friday, April 14, 2006 12:17 PM
Subject: Answer from the reporter...

It will be corrected tomorrow. Sorry it took so long. Deborah

Deborah Howell
Ombudsman
The Washington Post
****

From: Grant Smith
Sent: 04/27/2006 03:41 PM
To: Deborah C Howell <HowellDC@washpost.com>
Subject: Re: Answer from the reporter...

Dear Deborah C Howell,

Almost two weeks have now passed. Yesterday another journalist, possibly quoting Pincus's error, again misquoted the espionage statute:

http://www.newmediajournal.us/guest/silverberg/04262006.htm

Is it a priority for the WP to correct his error? If so, why so much delay?

Grant Smith
202-342-7325
****

Deborah C Howell <HowellDC@washpost.com> wrote:

Obviously, I need a neutral source. I'll try to find one. Deborah

Grant Smith

Subject: Re: Answer from the reporter...
04/14/2006 12:44
PM
****
To: "Deborah C Howell"
From: Grant Smith

Ms. Howell,

The Justice Department indictment was not inaccurate, rather
it has charged the defendants with violating *both* provisions
of the statute, rather than one or the other.

Walter Pincus's article clearly gives the reader an impression that
the law is more narrow than it actually is. Citing the indictment is
fine for the particulars of the case, in which the prosecution states
the defendants used classified information both "to the injury of
the United States" and to "advantage of a foreign nation".

However, Pincus was making a generalized statement about the
breadth of the statute. The Espionage Act statute states "to the injury of
the United States" *or* to "advantage of a foreign nation". This is
a major mistake. The statute is broader than Pincus stated it to be.

As I mentioned in previous correspondence, this citation error is
being propagated by researchers who rely on the Washington Post
as a "paper of record". I've invested energy in this correspondence
because I am a big fan of the newspaper, and believe it strives for
accuracy.

Now, behind the scenes, asking for a simple correction I get:

1 Denial "I was referring to the indictment" Pincus.
2. Appeal to Authority "Pincus is a Lawyer" Howell
3. Finger pointing "The indictment is wrong" Pincus

Why not just correct the record and demonstrate your commitment to
accuracy?

Grant Smith
****
From: "Deborah C Howell"

To:
Sent: Friday, April 14, 2006 12:17 PM
Subject: Answer from the reporter...
> Mr. Smith, here's Mr. Pincus' take on it. He also is a lawyer. Deborah
>Forwarded by Deborah C Howell/visitors/news/TWP on 04/14/2006 12:16
> PM -----
>
> Walter Pincus
> To: Deborah C
> Howell/visitors/news/TWP@WashPostMain
> 04/14/2006 11::10 cc:
> AM Subject: Re: Could you check
> this out? (Document link: Deborah C Howell)
>>
>>From a strict legal point a view, he is correct as to the way the law
>>reads and there is one case where the opinion makes that distinction.
>>However the indictment reads "...having reason to believe that said
>>information could be used to the injury of the United Stands and to the
>>advantage of any foreign nation, a violation of Title 18, United States Code,
>>Section 793 (d)." We based our language on the indictment, not the law.
>>That's what we said in the paper and I don't believe any correction is
>>needed. If this were a law review article I might put a footnote and say
>>the Justice Department indictment used inaccurate language. He should
>> take his argument to the prosecutors.
>>
>> Walter
> Deborah C Howell
> To: Walter
> Pincus/news/TWP@WashPostMain
> 04/13/2006 07:39 cc:
> PM Subject: Could you check this out?
>
> Walter, I figure that between your reporting and legal skills, you can
> answer this. Would you please copy me? Deborah
>
> Forwarded by Deborah C Howell/visitors/news/TWP on 04/13/2006 07:37
> PM -----"Grant Smith"
> Subject: Fw: When will we see a correction about the 04/13/2006 10:14
>Espionage Act error? AM Please respond to
> "Grant Smith"
> Dear Ms. Howell,
> I was reviewing the Corrections sections today, but did not see any
> correction of Walter Pincus' misquote of the 1917 Espionage Act.
> To the contrary, he continues to write about the Rosen and
> Weissman trial. Researchers following his contributions to this
> story via online databases will be misled by his reference
> to statutes, unless they are corrected.

> Is WAPO planning on issuing a correction? If not, why not?
>
> ----- Original Message -----
> From: "Grant Smith"
> To: "Walter Pincus"
> pincusw@washpost.com>
> Sent: Sunday, March 26, 2006 1:40 PM
> Subject: Re: Message via washingtonpost.com
>
>> Is a correction in the works?
>>
>> ----- Original Message -----
>> From: "Grant Smith"
>> To: "Walter Pincus"
>> Sent: Friday, March 24, 2006 7:34 PM
>> Subject: Re: Message via washingtonpost.com
>>> The *indictment* alleges Rosen and Weisman's actions
>>> injured the US and provided an advantage to a foreign nation. But
>>> the criminal statute states that *either* violation will do.
>>>
>>> Your article goes beyond the indictment and makes the incorrect
>>> generalization that to break the law and violate the Espionage Act, one
>>> must do what the AIPAC lobbyists allegedly did, injure AND advantage:
>>>"To break the law, the people involved must also believe the
>>> information "could be used to the injury of the United States and to the
>>> advantage of any foreign nation."
>>> That's simply not true. It may be a consolation that you're not the
>>> only one to have committed that error. The Washington Times did it as
>>> well (last sentence):
>>>
>>> www.washingtontimes.com/national/20060215-113838-3636r.htm
>>>
>>> I'm sure Lexis-Nexus is helping newsrooms across America to multiply
>>> the error. But shouldn't the WAPO accurately cite the criminal code, print
>>> a correction, and correct the record for American readers?
>>> Grant Smith
>>> ----- Original Message -----
>>> From: "Walter Pincus"
>>> To: "Grant Smith"
>>> Sent: Friday, March 24, 2006 7:00 PM
>>> Subject: RE: Message via washingtonpost.com
>>>
>>>>I took the definition from the Justice Department indictment of Count I.
>>>> ------ Original Message ------
>>>>
>>>> Grant Smith sent the following message:

>>>>
>>>> Your piece "Espionage Law's Merits Tied Into Ex-Lobbyists' Case"
>>>> contains a grave error.
>>>>
>>>> You state:
>>>>
>>>> "To break the law, the people involved must also believe the
>>>> information 'could be used to the injury of the United States and to the >>>>
advantage of any foreign nation.'"
>>>>
>>>> The law says no such thing. Rather it states:
>>>>
>>>> "Whoever, for the purpose of obtaining information respecting the
>>>> national defense with intent or reason to believe that the information is
>>>>to be used to the injury of the United States, *or* to the advantage of any
>>>>foreign nation"
>>>>
>>>> Both the Washington Post and the Washington Times have misquoted
>>>> the law. I'm not sure why, it may be consulted over the internet in
>>>> Findlaw or any other compilation of US Code.
>>>>
>>>> Can you issue a correction?
****

[194] August 2, 2007 faxed comments from Thomas W. Lippman to the author after he received a request to review the galley of "Foreign Agents".

[195] Judge T.S. Ellis, III, US vs. Steven J. Rosen and Keith Weissman, Memorandum Opinion, August 9, 2006

[196] Judge T.S. Ellis, III, US vs. Steven J. Rosen and Keith Weissman, Memorandum Opinion, August 9, 2006

[197] US Code Collection, Cornell University Law School, http://www.law.cornell.edu/uscode/html/uscode18/usc_sec_18_00000953----000-.html

[198] Christopher Drew and Michael Tackett, Chicago Tribune, December 10, 1992

[199] Council for the National Interest, 2004 http://www.cnionline.org/learn/polls/aipac/

[200] Jay Ward, Emergency Motion for Leave to Intervene with Respect to Proposed Closures of Trial Proceedings and Record, US vs. Steven J. Rosen and Keith Weissman

[201] Howard Kurtz, Washington Post, November 12, 2005

[202] Michael Wines, The New York Times, February 17, 1989

[203] George J. Church, Time Magazine, February 27, 1989

[204] Larry D. Thompson, Principles of Federal Prosecution of Business Organizations, January 20, 2003

[205] Judge T.S. Ellis, III, US vs. Steven J. Rosen and Keith Weissman, Memorandum Opinion, May 2007

[206] Judge T.S. Ellis, III, US vs. Steven J. Rosen and Keith Weissman, Memorandum Opinion, May 2007

[207] Judge T.S. Ellis, III, US vs. Steven J. Rosen and Keith Weissman, Memorandum Opinion, May 2007

[208] Judge T.S. Ellis, III, US vs. Steven J. Rosen and Keith Weissman, Memorandum Opinion, May 2007

[209] Judge T.S. Ellis, III, US vs. Steven J. Rosen and Keith Weissman, Memorandum Opinion, May 2007

[210] Judge T.S. Ellis, III, US vs. Steven J. Rosen and Keith Weissman, Memorandum Opinion, May 2007

[211] Russell Mokhiber, Corporate Crime Reporter, June 12, 2007

[212] Russell Mokhiber , Corporate Crime Reporter, June 12, 2007

[213] Peter Lattman, Wall Street Journal, June 25, 2007

[214] http://thomas.loc.gov/cgi-bin/query/z?c109:S.2831:

[215] http://thomas.loc.gov/cgi-bin/query/z?c109:S.2831:

[216] http://thomas.loc.gov/cgi-bin/query/z?c109:S.2831:

[217] Career campaign contributions from Pro-Israel PACs as compiled by the Washington Report on Middle East Affairs: Joe Biden, $101,007; Christopher Dodd, $182,928; Pete Dominici, $50,600; Lindsey Graham, $17,500; Chuck Grassley, $139,823; James Jeffords, $34,050; Joe Lieberman, $286,258; Charles Schumer, $56,635; Arlen Specter, $461,973.

[218] Thomas Stauffer, Washington Report on Near East Affairs, June 2003

[219] Judge T.S. Ellis, III, US vs. Steven J. Rosen and Keith Weissman, Memorandum Opinion, February 27, 2006

[220] Judge T.S. Ellis, III, US vs. Steven J. Rosen and Keith Weissman, Memorandum Opinion, February 27, 2006

[221] Washington Times, March 19, 2007

[222] USA Today, August 14, 2005

[223] Nathaniel Popper, The Forward, March 18, 2005

[224] http://www.irmep.org/11212005.htm

[225] DOJ employee Justin Dempsey's copy of a review galley was returned stamped "transferred to Anti-Trust." Review of court dockets reveals his current pursuit of anti-trust litigation.

[226] Internal AIPAC memo, cited in the Jerusalem Post, 24 August, 2004.

[227] Formerly Sec. 669 of the Foreign Assistance Act of 1961 as amended.

[228] According to the book *Manufacturing Consent*, "flak" can take the form of letters, bills before Congress, and complaints. It can be organized centrally or locally, by organizations or individuals. Although the book mentions flak-producing institutions organized to police the media, WINEP is a centralized front for flak designed to create and promote the Iran money-laundering issue as a way of laying the ground for a US military strike and diverting attention away from the massive global money laundering uncovered by Israeli prosecutor Talia Sason.

[229] Michael Jacobson, Jerusalem Post, June 30, 2007

[230] Levey also traveled to Israel in August 2007, as well as March 2007 and May 2006, according to the *Jerusalem Post*.

[231]

[232] United States Code, Section 18, Chapter 45, Expedition against a friendly nation

[233] Alvaro de Soto, End of Mission Report, United Nations, May 2007

[234] Alvaro de Soto, End of Mission Report, United Nations, May 2007

[235] http://www.newamericancentury.org/iraqclintonletter.htm

[236] Senate Foreign Relations Committee investigation into the Activities of Agents of Foreign Principals in the United States, pages 1716-1717, August 1, 1963

[237] Jacob Victor, Jewish Daily Forward, July 11, 2007

[238] Senate Foreign Relations Committee investigation into the Activities of Agents of Foreign Principals in the United States, pages 1716, August 1, 1963

[239] Elliot Abrams, page 60, Faith or Fear

[240] Elliot Abrams, page 72, Faith or Fear

[241] Elliot Abrams, page 67-68, Faith or Fear

[242] Elliot Abrams, page 129, Faith or Fear

[243] Elliot Abrams, page 137, Faith or Fear

[244] Elliot Abrams, pages 142-143, Faith or Fear

[245] Elliot Abrams, pages 157, Faith or Fear

[246] Alvaro de Soto, End of Mission Report, United Nations, May 2007

[247] Senate Foreign Relations Committee investigation into the Activities of Agents of Foreign Principals in the United States, page 1252, May 23, 1963

[248] Senate Foreign Relations Committee investigation into the Activities of Agents of Foreign Principals in the United States, page 1719, August 1, 1963

[249] George Washington, Farewell Address, September 19, 1796